Persuade People with Yo

Karen Mannering

79 606 982 6

I would like to dedicate this book to my father, Tony Bromage – the Master Marketeer!

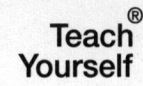

Persuade People
with Your Writing

Karen Mannering

Hodder Education

338 Euston Road, London NW1 3BH.

Hodder Education is an Hachette UK company

First published in UK 2012 by Hodder Education

First published in US 2012 by The McGraw-Hill Companies, Inc.

This edition published 2012

British Library Cataloguing in Publication Data: a catalogue record for this title is available from the British Library.

Library of Congress Catalog Card Number: on file.

10 9 8 7 6 5 4 3 2 1

www.hoddereducation.co.uk

Cover © jjayo - Fotolia

Typeset by Cenveo Publisher Services.

Printed in Great Britain by CPI Group (UK) Ltd, Croydon, CR0 4YY

Acknowledgements

I would like to thank my husband, Derek, who helped me with this book and never winced once.

Contents

Meet the author and introduction   xiii

Introduction   xv

1 Breaking through the myth barrier   1
Diagnostic test
"Everyone will think badly of me..."
"People will just say no..."
"Really nice people don't push themselves forward..."
"Everyone has everything they need"
"They probably know this already..."
"I don't want to sound like I have a job in sales..."
Focus points
Case studies
Next step

2 The new truths   15
Diagnostic test
"People like people..."
"Flattery will get you everywhere..."
"I'm sorry..."
"Come over to my side..."
"If I give you this..."
Taking action
Focus points
Case studies
Next step

3 Having a focus and an endgame   31
Diagnostic test
Can you have too much time?
Understanding your reader
Some time for research
Setting goals and deadlines
Write tight
Celebrating your success
Focus points
Case studies
Next step

4   Techniques that work   47
Diagnostic test
Selling the benefits
Emotionally speaking
Recommendations
Repetition
Solve the problem
Collaborating with the reader
Further techniques that can make a humungous difference
Focus points
Case studies
Next step

5   Persuasive language   67
Diagnostic test
Writing as a communication tool
The other side of writing
Making assumptions
The language we use
Analysing the written word
Starting with impact
Keeping it simple
Being consistent
Grouping
Focus points
Case studies
Next step

6   Writing to motivate   83
Diagnostic test
What is motivation?
Why creating motivation is important
Motivating words
Motivating phrases
The importance of appearance
Introducing motivational writing into your work
Focus points
Case studies
Next step

7   Presenting a cohesive argument   99
Diagnostic test
What is a cohesive argument?
Why and when should we be using one?
The advertorial

Structure is king
Don't forget to play with the words
You're leading me on!
Focus points
Case studies
Next step

8 Producing sales copy   113
Diagnostic test
Following AIDA
Creating a multiple sales strategy
Some truths about your customer
Why you should be selling yourself
Talk about the 'problem'
Set out the benefits
More techniques
Focus points
Case studies
Next step

9 Using persuasive techniques on the web   129
Diagnostic test
How visitors scan pages
Hooks and page links
Cut, rethink, cut, rethink
Blogs
E-zines
Focus points
Case studies
Next step

10 Using persuasive techniques at work   145
Diagnostic test
Writing a killer business plan
Appraisal and performance
Letters and emails
Presentations
Reports
Newsletters
Focus points
Case studies
Next step

Further reading   163
Helpful contacts   164
Index   165

Meet the Author and Introduction

Why do we sometimes give in to things we want or agree to actions that we really don't want to do? Could it be that someone else is pulling the strings?

It is an uncomfortable feeling that maybe we are not as free thinking and in control of our own decisions as we think we are. No one likes to think that they are being manipulated, but in many parts of life that is exactly what happens. Magazines are full of advertisements and good advice and we can feel ourselves changing our mind as somewhere a writer has sketched out what they think we should do.

In my career I have been on both sides of the fence. I have been persuaded by others and had to persuade clients, but this is far from being a dark art. In many cases you are simply retelling the story or setting out the benefits of the goods or services you offer.

Most of the techniques I have covered in this book are based on over 25 years of working with people in both buying and selling situations. I want to share them with you so that you can be more successful in whatever capacity you choose to deliver them.

By working through this book, you will be able to look critically at the range of techniques used to persuade others so that you can select the most appropriate technique for your own situation. There are numerous tips and tricks that will bring you improved results and also you will learn through following our two characters, Leonie and Paul, as they incorporate these techniques into their work.

Karen Mannering lives in Kent and is a specialist in people development with over 25 years' experience. She has worked in both the private and public sectors, has lectured at many seminars and has been quoted in national newspapers.

Karen has a degree in Psychology and a master's degree in Management Studies in addition to many skills-specific qualifications. She is a Fellow of the Institute of Personnel Development and a member of the British Psychological Society, the Chartered Management Institute and the Society of Women Writers and Journalists. Karen is also registered to use a wide range of psychometric tools to enhance her coaching.

Karen's enthusiasm for lifelong learning and people development, together with her background in management, results in a practical but humanistic approach to introducing training into the workplace. Karen also contributes regularly to several magazines and has written many books on aspects of self-development. Her website can be found at www.karenmannering.co.uk

Introduction

Nobody wants to feel sold to. However, the truth is that most of us are, every day. Forget about the scam that leaves us feeling foolish and taken in; I mean the casual advertising that we absorb, sometimes subliminally without realizing it. It is everywhere and why is it everywhere? Because it works.

I am not talking about some 'in your face' advertising campaign here, but advertising that is so subtle that you are left desperate for a product you never even knew you needed in the first place. Advertisers are paid millions to persuade you to take the very action that they want you to. The great thing is that, through this book, you can easily learn and use their techniques so that you can apply them to your writing, whether that is in a letter to a customer or asking the bank manager for an extension on your loan. The principles are the same: you want to persuade someone to take a certain action or react in a particular way.

We generally think that sales people are the only ones who can do this and furthermore that sales people are born. However, this is not really true. Anyone can learn these skills and develop their talents. There will be times when you don't get the reaction you expect and the important point here is to learn from these moments. You simply cannot get it right every time but you can hone your skills so that you hugely improve your chances of hitting the target more often than not.

Consider this...

As a little pre-exercise to this book, identify something that you bought recently based purely on the printed word. A book would be a good example. Perhaps you stood in the shop and read the back cover to gauge the contents. Now think, what made you take the decision to buy? Why did you choose this book and not one of the others with similar titles? Why did you decide to buy rather than borrow a copy from a friend or from a lending library?

Perhaps the book had one word on the back that captured your imagination, such as 'exciting' or 'compelling' and this made it stand out for you from the others that said 'enjoyable' or 'interesting'. Perhaps the book spoke to you in some way and you thought, 'this is just like my situation', or maybe there was a recommendation on the cover from someone you like or trust. These are all techniques that copywriters use to hook you into a sale. It is not that anyone is trying to trick you into buying – after all you are in the shop looking at books, so you were probably going to buy anyway – it is just that there are so many books on the market that each one needs to reach out in its own definable way.

Now think about how much effort you put into your written words. Do you dash them off because you simply don't have the time, or do you ponder each sentence long and hard? Email and electronic messaging has meant that we feel the need to rush our communication, but, if you have ever been in the situation where you have hurriedly sent a badly worded email and then lived to regret it (perhaps someone misinterpreted your meaning and took offence), you will know that it takes so long to redeem the situation that it would have been more prudent to have taken the time to consider the first message more carefully. Ah, the blessing of hindsight! When this happens, an interesting phenomenon occurs: for the next few days you read everything through twice and consider every detail, but it does not last long and soon you are dashing off those messages once again because habits like that are very hard to maintain in today's fast and hectic world – until the next time, of course (and the mistakes do tend to become larger!)

There is another way...

Instead of this unworkable fast and slow cycle, in which you inevitably fall down every so often and then spend ages in damage limitation and apologies, divide your written communication into tasks that are high risk and important and others that are low risk and less important. No sitting on the fence here!

Make two lists under the headings:

High-risk/important communication	Lower-risk/less important communication

Lower-risk and less important, regular communication can be done fast, whereas more high-risk, important written communication should be considered and allowed more time. Important communications are the tasks that will take you forward and are therefore worth investing your time in. Complete this task now with your current work load and see where you should be focussing your energy towards producing sharper and better-constructed copy. Throughout the book you can then work on these areas.

You might also like to consider at what time of day you are at your most creative. For example, if you are a morning person, then most of your high-risk communication should be designed and written at the time of day when you are most 'on the ball' if it is to reap the greatest rewards. It is well worth putting extra effort into the areas of your life where there will be the greatest payback, while allowing the other areas to come second on your list.

To help you achieve these goals, this book will take you on a journey that will enable you to consider and improve your written communication, so that your ideas have a greater chance of success and your career will flourish.

1

Breaking Through the Myth Barrier

Goal – To break through our misconceptions regarding writing persuasive copy.

Diagnostic test

Answer each question by choosing a number from 1 to 5. Nearer to 1 indicates that you feel this statement to be *false or incorrect* and nearer to 5 indicates that you feel it is *more likely to be true*.

People try to avoid sales people

Sales people are bad people

By being able to write persuasively I am tricking people

People won't like me if I seem to get what I want

I don't need writing techniques because I can get by on my own

Everybody already has what they need so I am wasting time introducing anything else

If I use 'sales talk' people will see through me

If I am good at my job I shouldn't need to persuade anyone to do anything – they will just trust my judgement

Genuine and honest people don't use persuasive writing techniques

If my attempt at using persuasive writing techniques is successful, I have cheated

Now add up your score and see what it says about you.

Result

35–50   You are afraid of using these techniques because you feel they will reflect badly on you. Every product or service you buy has, in some way, been sold to you by advertising copy – even the magazine or newspaper you buy has been designed to appeal to you. Does the editor feel bad about this? No! They are in a competitive market, where only the best survive – as are you! This chapter will help you to overcome your concerns or fears and help you to reframe how you see the role of persuasion marketing in your life. All work has some form of sales element. If you are not working with that correctly, there is a real possibility of you holding yourself back and not achieving as much as you could.

20–34   You have some mixed feelings about using persuasive writing. Perhaps you feel it is necessary but still fear that you don't want to be caught doing it? It pays to remember that people do not always know what is available to them and therefore it is your job to guide their attention to a service or product that can make their life easier. You are helping others to achieve their goals by making the outcomes and benefits more obvious. This chapter will help you to explore your personal fears and realize that persuasive writing is not an indictment of you as a person, but a skill that you can learn and practise, to gain better results in life.

Below 20   You understand fully that sales people are not 'bad' and that everyone has problems that need solutions. However, you can have the most amazing solution in the world but nobody will take notice until they are persuaded to listen. As persuasive writers, we need to use our skills to enable readers to access those solutions. This chapter will help you to understand how others may see the role of persuasive writing and will therefore help you to clarify your own thoughts on the subject.

Successful persuasive writing can spark extreme interest and excitement in some people and extreme concern in others. For some, it is the key to unlock the door to winning sales letters and increased returns – but to others it may spell manipulation and coercion.

Try it now

Ask approximately ten people you know how they feel about persuasive writing and whether their thoughts would change if they were able to write more persuasively themselves.

If you undertook the above action you are likely to find that most people like the idea of being able to persuade other people but don't like the idea of being persuaded themselves! Why is this? Probably because, if you felt you had been persuaded to undertake some action, then it automatically cannot be the action you would have chosen to take, can it? Surely there must have been some mind control, mesmerism or hypnosis involved? They fear that their own free will has been removed from them and some trickery has been introduced. This results in instant suspicion and causes the person to attempt to distance themselves from the source as far as possible, when in fact nothing can be further from the truth.

But what about if you are only persuading them to do the very thing they were going to do anyway? In this situation you are surely only speeding up the decision that they were going to take. Consider this: if someone is reading a magazine on cookery, I think we can assume that they are interested in cookery and probably had every intention of cooking something from the magazine at some point in their life. Therefore a writer using persuasive writing within the magazine to highlight an offer is not really taking advantage of you in a weak situation. Let's take this example further: if someone walks into a showroom displaying new cars I think it fair to assume that they probably are at least a little interested in buying a new car (after all, it is not a thing we do just because we have time on our hands). Therefore, if the sales professional hands them some advertising copy about the car and attempts to speak to them about it, I think we can take the view that they are trying to help them by bringing the inevitable purchase forward, and in the long run, waste less of their time.

 Try it now

Reflect on how many times you have wasted time simply procrastinating and pondering on a decision that, in the back of your mind, you know you are going to take anyway. (For example, have you ever seen an item of clothing you liked, did not make the decision and then had to go back the next day to buy it – even though it meant rushing off after work or back into town?) How many hours of your life could have been saved had someone just encouraged you to take action in the first place?

Your fear of being 'sold to' may seem completely logical to you but it actually says less about the power of the writer than about how you feel about yourself. Do you really feel that you have no self-will to refuse offers and ideas that you do not want? Of course not! It is just a myth that persuasive writing has some kind of power over us. The truth is that sometimes we need that little nudge to take an action that we were going to take anyway, but felt we needed more evidence.

Remember this

Persuasive writing is not simply about selling. It is helping the reader to have confidence to buy the object or service that they were probably going to buy anyway.

Authors use persuasive writing all the time to engage us with their characters. Haven't you felt so sucked into a story that you simply must put other tasks aside so that you can finish it?

While we are myth-busting, let's look at some other myths that get in the way of us producing great persuasive writing:

'Everyone will think badly of me...'

At the very centre of our being we all love to be liked.

Try it now

What does 'being liked' mean to you? Make a list of the signs that show you how much you are liked.

You may have had difficulty undertaking that activity because even admitting that we look for the signs that we are liked can feel uncomfortable. How many of the items you wrote down are about how you feel about yourself and how many are attributed to the feelings and approbation of others? We cannot have any control over the feelings of others but even so we cannot deny that being liked by other people makes us feel warm and wanted – lovely qualities that we want to encourage. Conversely the opposite is also true: very few people would want to feel out in the cold and alienated – but would they feel suspicious of you just because you are using tools and techniques that can help them and bring you more business? No. I believe not.

Let me be straight here: we are not using mind-bending techniques in this book. We are not trying to persuade someone against their will or force them to do anything they do not want to do. We are just presenting the benefits and describing the product in a way that shows it off to its advantage, in the same way that you would accessorize an outfit to emphasize certain aspects of it, or select a style of clothing that shows your physique to its best advantage.

Rather than thinking badly of you, I believe that your colleagues are more likely to be in awe of you, in the same way that we are in awe of a make-up artist or an interior designer who manages to create something wonderful from an ordinary person or room. You need to start thinking of yourself as an artist – an artist with words!

'People will just say no...'

And they are entitled to do that. A high proportion of advertising material hits the waste bin before anyone has even read it. However, you can increase your chances of your message being read by considering certain techniques that draw the eye or catch the attention of the reader.

Try it now

Consider what catches your eye in your local supermarket. Tick the deals below that you find most interesting. Which ones catch your attention?

* Buy one get one free
* FREE GIFT
* 50% extra
* Half price
* Money back
* Token included
* 3 for 2
* Lucky number included

We are so familiar with these offers that we accept and expect them. Therefore we are very in tune with being offered a deal of this type and have come to expect it. This form of persuasive writing is now being used in many lines of business (such as jewellery stores) whereas once it was the preserve of supermarkets. This means that people are becoming familiar with this language and are therefore less likely to say no outright and more likely to be intrigued.

Remember this

Ideas such as this need not be confined to selling goods in shops. If you want to write a memo to your boss asking them to consider you moving towards job sharing in the future, how about heading the memo 'Buy one get one free' or 'Get two for the price of one'? That just might raise a smile at the same time as introducing an important point.

However, let's just tackle this issue of someone saying no, head on. Some people *will* say no. Even if you stood in the street offering people passing by free money, some people would say no. This says more about them than you. Perhaps they have been cheated before, perhaps they are nervous of their own ability to refuse politely, perhaps they have been cornered in the past – you can't know any of this and so don't try to guess. You can only put your idea forward, or set your wares on the table, and hope that someone is intrigued enough to find out a little more. Then, if your idea or offer is a good one, they will feel compelled to act favourably towards it, perhaps moving you to the next stage of speaking with them.

'Really nice people don't push themselves forward...'

Is this true? I don't think so. Holding back on a great idea just to appear nice does not sound very clever to me, but, again, I can see that we are told these myths when we are young and they stick with us for the rest of our lives. Perhaps the overconfident child was told this to encourage them to hold back, but there is a huge difference between pushing in front of someone in a queue (not nice behaviour) and pushing forward in your career (very acceptable behaviour).

Mark the following as either pushing (P) or helpful (H):

> 'Would you like to buy any batteries to go with this toy?'

> A label that says 'Buy this nightdress and have a matching wrap for half price'.

> A sign that reads 'If quality is what you value – buy this product now'.

> 'Would you like to increase your meal to a "Bonus" for an additional 50 pence?'

I think you would agree that none of these would send you into a tirade at either the assistant or the store manager and none of these comments would classify the person who wrote them as 'nice' or 'horrible'. And yet there is still this pervading myth that you are pushing something that another person does not want. If this is a real concern for you, then thankfully there is a midway point. Simply ask yourself regularly, are you doing this to be helpful to the customer? If the answer is yes, then in no way are you being pushy or unpleasant.

(For the record, there are really nice people in every strata of society – just as there are rotters! This is not dependent on their jobs or their ability to present material in a winning way. I'm afraid that those traits are a mixture of life experience, personality and values, together with how we wish to present ourselves – nothing at all to do with writing successful and persuasive copy.)

Key idea

Really nice people are those who help their friends and recommend goods and ideas that help friends to live easier lives.

'Everyone has everything they need'

It is true that many of us are indeed well catered for in life and many people today do have all that they need – but is it all that they want? New products come out every day to satisfy the latest desire and some of them are merely updates on the traditional model. Let's take a kitchen mop as an example.

In the absence of one that actually climbs out of the cupboard and mops up by itself, there are many (very similar) mops on the market – all promising to be the best. New models are launched every day to meet the constant need for mops and also our need for invention. Every home may indeed have a mop, but do they have the latest technology in mops? Do they have the lightest mop that does the work in half the time? Even if you have invented the 'King of Mops', persuading others to buy it and take a risk on your product needs careful copy – after all, you are competing in a very saturated market – but it can be done, even in the area of kitchen essentials.

Speaking of kitchens, every year I go on holiday and stay in a holiday home. I am always struck by the sparseness of kitchen utensils and bowls and so forth. However, strangely enough, we manage very well with what is supplied and I have never felt the need to go out and buy any additional items. When I get home, I am surprised by the vast amount I have accumulated in my kitchen – and I am sure that I would tell you that I absolutely need every item. The truth is somewhat different. I don't actually need them but each item makes one job or another a little easier (and some were recommended by a TV chef – persuasive language!). In other words I bought them because I wanted them, I desired them and they make me feel professional in my kitchen.

If you are ever concerned by the thought that everyone has the product or service you are going to write for, consider the humble paper clip. Who buys them? Where do they go? They don't wear out like pens, or snap like elastic bands – and so surely we don't need any more? Yet thousands of boxes are sold and bought every day. There is an insatiable desire for new items and novelty in addition to functional items that we use every day. Ladies, very few of us actually *need* that new pair of shoes or handbag but we surely want them!

Key idea

We desire items for many different reasons (some of them quite complex such as because the item makes us feel better) and, if we are not buying them from you, we will buy them elsewhere. Therefore, it may as well be from you.

'They probably know all this already...'

As part of my work providing presentations and training programmes, I speak to thousands of people. The biggest mistake I can make is to assume that everyone knows the topic already or has the same level of knowledge as myself. Put simply, they don't. Some people will know nothing, others very little, and from then onwards there is a graduating scale of knowledge, but I cannot assume that people 'probably know the background to this'. I am sure you can see where I am coming from on this one. When you write persuasive copy you need to strike a balance between educating the reader and building their confidence to take action. If you assume that everyone knows just what you are going to say, then you will never write anything.

Example: Take a good look at people choosing a cleaning product in a supermarket. Watch their behaviour. If they know what they are going to buy, they go straight to the product (because they know where it tends to be in the shop, as they buy it regularly) and they put it straight in their basket. Job done – they are not looking to change product, unless something happens such as their current product fails to perform, or some new item catches their eye in an advertising campaign. So let's ignore them for now. Now look at the behaviour of the person who does not know exactly what they want to buy. They start to pick up different products and read the labels. One label reads:

> Gets rid of stubborn stains on
>
> Carpets
>
> All flooring
>
> All soft furnishings

Another label reads:

> This is really good – and it works!

Given that someone had dropped some red wine on their carpet last night, which one do you think most people would buy?

Most people would go for the first example, because the label tells you that it will answer your *specific* need. The other is asking you to extend a leap of faith that the product will actually be good in the area you need it to be. The second example also assumes that you probably know what the product does already – but you don't. The person picking up these products will read about approximately four products before selecting their choice and each time they will read the label – even if they are in the carpet-cleaning section of the supermarket. From those labels they are looking to select the right product for their problem and so assuming that they know what to buy is a lost opportunity.

Key idea

Very often we are too close to our own topic and assume too much. Assume nothing and then you start with a clean slate upon which to design your own message.

'I don't want to sound like I have a job in sales...'

Essentially everyone has a job in sales. Most organizations rely on sales of either goods or services to survive. After all, you have what others want, whether that be a commodity, a service or some information. Never underestimate how much another person will pay for information that saves them time or provides a shorter route to success – and you could be the key to that information.

You may not have gone into a job that is specifically sales, but be in no doubt that sales and selling is as much a part of your job as anything else you do. Every time you speak to a client you are 'selling the company' in some way and building their trust and every time you speak to your manager or colleagues you are 'selling you'. That is part of the bond of trust that we each sell to each other. When you say to a colleague, 'I will take that off you and deal with it later', you are asking them to trust you in two ways:

▶ to trust that the job will be done in the first instance and

▶ that you will do it in a professional manner that fits with the organization.

Remember this

Everyone has a job in sales in that they help organize and promote the business. However, no one would think that, because you can write persuasive copy, you necessarily work in the sales department.

Focus points

Persuasive writing has a number of myths attached to it.

When you write persuasively you are, in many instances, just bringing forward the inevitable action, therefore saving everyone time.

Everyone is persuasive to some extent in their lives. If you have ever tried to get someone to take you to the movies rather than go shopping, you were using persuasive language.

Persuasive writing is a skill; everyone can learn to structure their writing to have greater impact.

You do not have to be 'in sales' to increase this skill.

Case studies

Throughout this book we will be following Leonie and Paul in their quest to improve their persuasive writing.

Leonie is out of work. She wants to get a job in an office but seems to be getting nowhere, especially as she was not even called for an interview at her last attempt. She realizes that the job market is very competitive at the moment and the feedback from her last application was that they were looking for someone who 'stood out from the crowd'. Leonie is puzzled by this because she has done quite a few interesting things in her life and put them at the bottom of her CV, thinking that they might give her the edge. She goes back and looks at her application letter. It really says very little about her best points and just refers them to her (attached) CV. She realizes that this was an opportunity wasted. They probably did not even get as far as looking at the CV, let alone the bottom of page 2. Her self-promotion should have been in the covering letter. When she phoned up for feedback the human resources person told her that there is another similar job coming up at the same company next month and to look out for it if she is still interested. Leonie wants to give it a go and decides to give the letter her full attention. She does not mind going 'back to the drawing board' because she knows that every opportunity is precious, and that, if her letter and CV combination did not work last time, there is very little point in presenting the next one in the same way. She realizes that, to make change happen, something has to change – and she decides it is her CV and letter.

Paul works at Pan Haulage, a family-owned company. He has been there since leaving school and has worked his way up from tea-boy to office manager. He has had no training except for watching others and learning how the business works. The fact that it is a family business means that many of the decisions are taken within the family of Bill Pan (the owner), Melissa (his wife and secretary) and their children, Thomas (who is just leaving school and will be attending college) and Lizzie (10 years old). Old Mr Pan, who started the business 50 years ago, is still very much a part of the business. Paul has learned that he has to really understand the dynamics of the family *and* the business if he is to make things happen at Pan Haulage. The future looks tough in the haulage industry and Paul recognizes that things cannot go on as before. He has ideas but he needs to be more persuasive if he is to implement any of them. Mr Pan has always done things a certain way and Paul decided that, if he is to persuade Bill even to consider some of his observations, he will have to look at ways in which he can start to present his ideas. Paul has never written sales copy or undertaken a presentation in his entire life, but he reasons that it is never too late to learn – and these could be useful skills for the future too.

Next step

As you have been working through the 'Diagnostic test' and the 'Try it now' sections you will have a good appraisal of how comfortable you feel about writing persuasively. This chapter looked at some of the myths that surround successful persuasive writing and I hope helped to dispel many of them. You have also met Leonie and Paul and you will see throughout this book how they use their skills to develop effective techniques. In the following chapter we will be looking at more helpful truths that can hold the key to producing winning copy.

2

The New Truths

Goal – To set out some new rules about how we will work together.

Diagnostic test

Answer each question by choosing a number from 1 to 5. Nearer to 1 indicates that you feel this statement to be *false or incorrect* and nearer to 5 indicates that you feel it is *more likely to be true*.

I believe that people like people

I love to be liked

I don't mind apologizing if I have done something wrong

I believe there is no limit to what people can achieve in life

If people like us they will want to help us

I believe that it is fine if we both benefit from some situation or decision

If I don't ask people to trust me I could be missing a trick

I am proud when my name goes alongside a project

I am comfortable with responsibility

I believe that people like me

Now add up your score and see what it says about you.

Result

35–50   You have a very open and trusting relationship with others. It is very likely that other people want to work with you and be in your team. However, just a word of warning. Overconfident behaviour can sometimes be interpreted as showing off. No one should want to knock your confidence, but we always need to consider how our behaviour affects others, and, if it is a problem, then we need to reconsider how we redress any balance. These new truths will help you to place this in perspective.

20–34   Were there some statements you agreed with and others you did not? Or did you select a midway point on each? If it was the latter I would like you to stop sitting on the fence and do the Diagnostic test again, but this time striking only to the left or right.

If you had a spread of answers then I suggest that there are some areas of self-confidence in which you are less comfortable. Look at the questions where you scored towards 5 and ask yourself if there are areas of your life where you could make big changes to your thinking. This chapter can help you consider how you think about yourself and how this affects your behaviour, with both customers and colleagues.

Below 20   Are you possibly a pessimist? Have you had a bad experience with people in the past? It seems that you do not feel that people trust you or want you to do well. If you think like this, for whatever reason, you could be creating blocks that are stopping you from achieving the things you want in life. Most jobs today require team work and/or project work and you may need to think through how you work with people if you feel that they do not trust you. The other issue may be your behaviour. If you do not feel trusted by others this may manifest itself through your behaviour and how you act. Those who do not like or trust others may become withdrawn, a behaviour that is picked up by others. I hope this chapter gives you further ideas.

As the previous chapter set out to dispel myths, we need to fill the void left by them, through the creation of some new truths about the art of persuasive writing and incorporating it into our daily lives.

Try it now

Grab a piece of paper and a pen and, considering the myths in the previous chapter, what would you consider to be the counter truths? Second, how can knowing these truths help you?

One of the great outcomes of dispelling myths and accepting new counter truths is that you can now start to open up to a new way of working and thinking – and, when you see that new way delivering results, you can appreciate its power. When you know and accept the truth about persuasive writing, you will see how it can help you in all areas of your life, whether you want to write an advertisement for a product or a letter of introduction for yourself. You can use persuasive writing for charity work, in your personal life and in your main employment. You can use it to help schools and hospitals raise funds and for conservation projects – in fact you can use it anywhere and in any situation. At this point you are possibly wondering why it is not taught everywhere. Well, perhaps it should be, but for now it isn't and that gives you the advantage. You are the one reading this book and you are the one benefitting from this knowledge and experience. If you choose to share your skills at a later date, then that is up to you, but, for now, concentrate on honing those skills and accept the advantages they bring.

Remember this

These skills can bring you great advantage and you need to think about how and where you feel comfortable using them. Like everything in life, they can be used positively or negatively and the way in which they are used says something distinct about you.

With knowledge comes responsibility and so it is helpful to think through where you were hoping to use these skills. With whom? To what end? Remember that your answers will reveal a great deal about yourself.

Now let's have a look at some of the new truths that it pays to remember when writing persuasively:

'People like people...'

Humans are incredibly social creatures. Yes, really! Even those who like to keep themselves to themselves enjoy personal connections from time to time. We can be like heat-seeking missiles, searching out others and making connections – especially when we feel alone or in a slightly tense situation.

Weddings or parties are great for observing this in action, especially ones where you don't really know many people and you are all thrown together for a significant number of hours. As you mingle, you try to find someone with whom you can make a connection; you grapple to find any slight topic on which you can create a shared conversation. Sport is always a good one, or holidays. "I went to the Greek isles last year, have you been? Yes? Oh, which ones did you visit?" – and we are off and running. Once we have found that common factor, we will hang everything else on it, but this is more than a conversation about Greece. It is by making these connections and creating similarity that we can start to feel comfortable and it is only when we feel comfortable that we can then branch out into expressing our opinions or taking the conversation into a more ambitious or unusual direction. Therefore, it is not surprising that later that night you are able to be more free in your opinions: "Sport? I hate it!"

Try it now

Remember the last wedding or party you attended. What was your behaviour? Did you try to find someone with whom you had a connection (even if it was only somebody who knew someone else you know)? If you did then you were just like most of the human race – all trying to make connections.

Knowing that people like people can be very helpful to us as writers, because writers need to connect with their readers. The only difference is that writers need to do it through words on paper (or through some other textual medium) rather than by talking. When we know that people like us, our writing becomes less constrained and we feel more able to reveal our personalities. We can let our writing flow like a conversation and we don't feel judged.

When we feel connected to people we are also able to recommend things to them and freely accept recommendations from others. For example, imagine that you are in the pub one evening and you start talking to someone at the bar and you find out that you have several friends in common. Throughout the evening the talk moves onto other subjects such as which Internet provider you use, which power supplier you chose and where would be a good place to go on holiday. You find yourself giving and accepting ideas, you offer advice and you listen to recommendations, and you are likely to continue thinking about your conversation for days afterwards. If you get on especially well, the connection is good and you like the subjects you discussed, you might decide to look up some of these companies or ideas the following day. Notice that I am suggesting here that it is the conversation you had and the recommendation that sets you off searching. You went searching not just because it sounds like a good idea, but because someone has suggested or recommended it to you. Such is the power of personal recommendation from someone with which we have a connection – however slight.

How does this transfer to writing? When we write persuasively we need to make it as easy as possible for the reader to develop that connection with us, so that, when we lead our written 'conversation' in a different direction, they want to accompany us, rather than put the copy down.

Key idea

Many people follow the antics of a celebrity journalist who describes their day in such a way that the reader is at the same time fascinated and yet somewhat shocked. Most newspapers carry such a column, as they are very popular. The reader really feels not only that they identify with the character but also that they are their friend. This is why celebrity endorsements are very successful. After all, if your friend recommended a product to you, you would want to try it, wouldn't you? – and we all like to think we could be friends with the stars.

'Flattery will get you everywhere...'

We like to be liked, and flattery is wonderful, unless you feel you are being made a fool of – then it turns sour. Genuine flattery is enjoyed by most people – yes, even those who seem amused or unaffected by it. It provides approbation and signifies that we make good choices. For example, if you comment favourably on another person's outfit, you are not just saying the equivalent of 'I like your clothes'; you are really transmitting a number of other messages such as:

Your clothes are the right choice for today (you have taste).

Your clothes have appeal (you have style).

Your clothes suit your body shape (they look great because you look great).

I would choose (and possibly covet) what you are wearing.

I like you.

Hold on, what was that last one? 'I like you' – that can't be right; after all it is a comment that is nothing to do with the clothes! But that is exactly the point. When we flatter someone, we are not necessarily showing them that we approve of the thing that we are commenting on; it also sends messages of personal approval. After all, if we did not care about someone we would simply not comment or engage. Many a personal relationship or friendship has begun with a general comment such as 'I like your shoes'; a comment that is apparently nothing to do with liking the person, but is more than about the shoes!

However, we also have to consider when flattery is false. Strangely, we all seem to have a small antenna that is quite adept at knowing when we receive a comment that does not feel genuine. We react very strongly to it, often translating the favourable comment into an insult. It is therefore very important to be genuine in your comments and not leave room for confusion.

This is very important for the writer. If you want to persuade someone with your writing, being complimentary is very effective – but please err on the side of caution and ask a colleague to read through your text as you do not want to turn your readers off by using clumsy prose.

Key idea

Flattery used with a light touch: **'You know how it is when you reach the age where you know so much more, when you become a stronger person, a more definite you...'** (many people will identify with this as it centres on the wisdom of years).

False flattery: **'You know you look great. Look in the mirror, what a beautiful person you are...'** (very few people will identify with this approach because it only applies to people who think themselves beautiful and that can appear very shallow – many people would stop reading at that point).

Flattery can also be about consistency and regularity and should be used lightly (as in the first example above). Constant flattery may feel good at first but soon wears the reader down and they start to feel that there is a strong possibility that you are making fun of them. Also, if the comments are inconsistent, the reader may become suspicious.

Try it now

What flattery do you find acceptable and what do you find too much? Think about your own experiences: when do you know that someone is genuinely flattering you? What might make you think otherwise? What can you learn about this for your own writing?

'I'm sorry...'

We all make mistakes. Unfortunately, it is inevitable that we say and do things that we later regret or learn were incorrect. However uncomfortable the situation, it is how we deal with this that redeems us in the eyes of others. Do you hold your head high, brazen it out and bluster on regardless – after all, everyone will soon forget your misdemeanour – or do you show your contrition and risk looking a little foolish and vulnerable? Only you can choose the right approach in each situation, but over and over evidence shows that people favour the truly contrite. Notice that I say here the *truly* contrite, not those who just apologise but seem to learn nothing from the situation.

How can this be? Everyone loves a winner, right? That must mean that they hate a loser! Not so. When someone puts their hand up to confess they are often perceived as brave: they are demonstrating strength and honesty and they are showing a willingness to put things right. By apologizing you are also asking others to accept you again and give you another try, thereby engaging them with your plight (because we have all been there; none of us are faultless). With all that on your side, how could you lose?

In fact, apologizing is so effective in bringing people on to your side that many writers of persuasive text will even apologize when they have not done anything! Only last week I received an email containing the strap line: 'Will you forgive me?' How could I resist opening it? The writer was simply apologizing for having such a great product that they wanted to get it out to everyone as soon as possible. They were apologizing for bothering me with something they simply could not keep to themselves. Did I want to know what that was? You bet – very persuasive. If something is so important that someone apologizes to me for crashing in on my time, I need to know about it, don't I?

This technique can be incorporated into any sales copy and many writers use it as a hook to engage with people quickly and demonstrate vulnerability.

Key idea

People love vulnerability – it makes them feel stronger by comparison. Whether you are apologizing for a genuine mistake or using it as an interesting hook for your readers, ensure that it is sincere and readers will pay you back with their attention and understanding.

'Come over to my side...'

Have you ever been described as a leading light, a key figure, an influencer, a person with presence? If so, then you will already be aware of your own personal magnetism. Some people simply have the ability to engage and encourage others just by being in the room – and we all just long to be in their gang. There is a huge amount of power in reflective light. Has anyone ever told you how they went to the wedding of that minor celebrity or their cousin is roadie to a particular group? They could just be informing you about their lives or family but it is more likely that they are hoping to impress you with their connections. People like connections and to be alongside someone with gravitas.

In fact, it is here that you can be at your most persuasive. If people want to identify themselves with you, they will want a part of whatever you are offering. They will want to shop at the same shops and buy the same brands. This is why celebrity endorsements for products and services are so lucrative. People identify with celebrities and want to be in their 'gang'. They do this by adopting an identical style, which may include wearing similar clothes and/or adopting their ideas and opinions. Once people are followers, it is then simple for the celebrity to lead them in any direction they want. For example, you may have been attracted to a celebrity because of their music but, as you come to like them more, you will want to dress like them or show that you are a fan by wearing advertising t-shirts and so forth. When they tweet that they use a certain brand of face cream, you rush out to buy it. Now hold on a minute! Buying a face cream is a long way from liking their music. We don't even know what type of skin they have and we seem to have leapt from liking their music to adopting their facial routine – how can that be? Surely the two are not connected? But advertisers do this all the time and they are extremely successful. They understand the power of aligning any product with a celebrity and if they can build in characteristics so much the better; for example, using someone known for their maturity, integrity and honesty to front a campaign for health insurance aimed at the over-55s.

What does this mean to you? Have you thought about your own image? What do you have that people could adopt or want? How could they show you that they are in your 'gang'? How would you know that you have these followers?

Key idea

By developing a persona that people want to live alongside you are instantly in a position of influence. This technique is not limited to celebrities. Think about whom you admire at work or in other spheres of life. Have you copied their clothes? Are they a strong influence? Are other people already watching and copying you?

'If I give you this...'

When we offer to help or bestow a favour we usually do so in the (often unspoken) belief that the favour will be returned, and very often it is. This is the power of reciprocity, the social law that states that, if one person bestows a favour or undertakes a deed for another person, then at some point the deed will be reciprocated in some way.

You might see this at work. 'I covered for you last Friday lunchtime and so now could you return the favour by covering for me on Wednesday and Thursday lunchtime?' Sound familiar? One minute someone helped you out of a fix and the next you appear to be in their debt (and sometimes the repayment terms are higher than the initial investment).

Notice that this 'arrangement' had not been agreed in advance; that would have been more like bartering or negotiation, and of course, had the terms been set out in advance, you might not have accepted giving two days' cover in return for one – hopefully you would have struck out for a better deal! No, this is more sneaky, with one person offering to cover for you at the time with the implication that they would be happy just to do that – and only later letting you know that you should think in terms of a generous repayment. And do we repay? Of course we do, because that is being kind and polite and society works only if we all help each other.

How can this law of reciprocity help us as persuasive writers? Well, we can call in some favours of our own. How can we do that when we don't actually know the customers personally? Try this sales copy:

> Yesterday I gave you three valuable tips to increase sales. I gave them away as a favour to you and I have another gift for you today, five knockout tips for keeping the customers you already have happy and constantly returning to you. Although these tips are also free I know that you would never mind me asking something of you. I want to create a personal development programme that meets your every need and so I want you to tell me three of your largest problems with clients. I want those knotty problems, the ones that stink and that staff have difficulty dealing with...

OK, two free gifts in return for some information – would you consider that a good deal? Would you reciprocate and send in the information? It all seems pretty harmless and you have been given some useful tips. Most people would find this a reasonable deal. You may be wondering how this information would help the writer, but it is invaluable! This persuasive writer will use that information to create a staff development programme that now exactly meets the reader's needs (because they told the writer what they wanted) and will then sell the package back to their audience. *And* the writer now also has the list of recipients who replied – the people most likely to be interested in the programme because they originally identified the problems. Their next email contact will probably now say something along the lines of:

> **Thank you to everyone who so kindly responded. You helped me enormously and now I would like to help you in return. I have designed a new programme that you can help me pilot at a very special price. Your staff will gain the benefit of a programme specifically designed to suit your industry needs and as a very special thank you, I will be offering it to you, for one month only at...**

We are back to reciprocity again. Notice that the writer is asking the reader for help once again because they have now designed something that they believe the reader wants. They are effectively saying that, because you responded last time, you are saying you need and want this programme. It is a persuasive technique that is used on many Internet sites to great effect.

Remember this

Reciprocity is effective when you have built a relationship with your customers and you are not asking for very much – perhaps just a small bit of information. They feel obliged to provide you with some simple information mainly because they like you and buy into that relationship.

Taking action

Dare we ever ask our readers to actively do something? You may feel that is a little like putting pressure on. In fact, to you it may seem a bit bossy and unbelievably cheeky to command the reader to 'Go on, do it! Do it NOW', but in many instances that is exactly what we need the reader to do. Indeed in some instances, when people dither, it is exactly what they want us to do too.

Remember what we said earlier: at this point the reader is engaged sufficiently to have continued reading your message – they would have stopped by now if they had not been, at the very least, curious what you are going to suggest. However, they may not actually know what the next step is, unless the writer guides them skilfully. Without that final step the reader can be left dangling, thinking 'Well that was all very well and I am interested but I don't know what I am supposed to do.'

Imagine that you have just seen the most amazing product either on the television or in an advertisement, but you are not told where to obtain this product. Are you going to go looking for it? Do you have all the time in the world to research it further? If you have then you are very fortunate because most people don't, and, furthermore, by now they will be frustrated and bored and may not even bother to buy it if they then see it in a shop, because after such frustrated efforts it is now associated with negative thoughts.

It is therefore essential that we spell out this final step whether that be in an Internet advert requesting the reader to purchase, for example:

Click here to BUY NOW at this special price

or in a letter asking the reader to send specific information:

We cannot proceed with your claim unless you can provide us with your driving licence or some other photographic proof of identity. We need these documents IMMEDIATELY to further your claim.

(Notice the repetition in the second example. The two sentences have much the same meaning but the power is in the repetition. I will feature how to use repetition with effect later in this book).

Remember this

Don't expect the customer to take action unless you specifically invite them to do so. Everyone leads busy lives. If they walk away from your writing, thinking 'maybe I will later' – they rarely do. They have invested their valuable time in reading your words and therefore you can assume they are interested enough to want to find out more.

Focus points

Persuasive writing does have a number of myths attached to it, but it also has truths that can help us to gauge and work with our audience.

People like to make connections with other people, they want to find out more about you, so do not be afraid to start relationship building early on.

Most people react well to flattery as long as it is genuine, sincere and warmly meant.

Making a mistake should not spell the end of business for persuasive writers because they know that, if they apologize in the right way, they can win the customer back.

The power of reciprocity means that, if I am willing to give something, then the other person is also likely to reciprocate.

Case studies

How are Leonie and Paul doing? Let's take a look.

Leonie decides to dedicate a whole day to sorting out the problem with her CV. However, she cannot shake off the concern that a CV should just contain facts. Perhaps she should start on the letter? She is a bit confused. Fortunately, her sister's boyfriend has just started work with a recruitment agency and has offered Leonie an hour of his time. He explains that, although Leonie is correct that her CV should contain facts, it also has to be engaging and show Leonie in her best light. That does not mean lying but it does mean emphasizing her key skills and showcasing what she can do – even if that means creating a separate CV for every job she applies for (because they will each have a slightly different focus). He also explains that the covering letter should be brief but pick out a few of Leonie's leading skills so that they catch the eye of the reader and invite them to take a further look. He tells Leonie to go back to the job description and highlight what she thinks are the most important aspects of the job and to make sure the covering letter includes these. Finally, he points out that the letter is there to gain engagement and the CV provides facts on where she has worked and what she did, but there is one aspect missing: who Leonie is as a person. He suggests she consider including a Personal Profile that actually sells Leonie as a person. This is a lot to take in but Leonie agrees that it does cover all angles and could look very professional. She goes away to make notes and plan her new layout.

Paul was feeling a little daunted but he now realizes that there is a lot about persuasive writing that he had not thought about. It actually is a very positive way to work and operate and he decides to list all the areas of business life in which he can use this skill. He originally thought it would be useful only for dealing with Mr Pan and his family, but now he realizes that he can use it with staff and also some of the advertising copy. He has noticed just recently that Pan Haulage has always promoted the fact that it is a family business, but in a very quiet way. Pan Haulage needs to promote itself in line with modern ideas and values and at the moment communities are backing local family businesses. That means that they are also interested in the other factors that surround a family business such as price, locality, history, service and many more. The public may also need it spelling out to them what Pan Haulage could do for them and possibly even asking for their support. Paul starts to get excited because he can see that he will be able to incorporate persuasive writing into just about all aspects of his work.

Next step

As you have been working through the 'Diagnostic test' and the 'Try it now' sections you will now begin to see that human nature has some truths that we, as persuasive writers, can work with. This chapter also covered that all-important final step: asking the customer to take action. If we run away from this, our reader may too and therefore it is essential that we plan our message and know exactly what we are asking the reader to do. In the following chapter we will be doing just that as we start to shape our goals more closely to ensure the result we want and expect.

3

Having a Focus
and an Endgame

Goal – to focus the writer on the required outcome and help you to avoid mistakes.

Diagnostic test

Answer each question by choosing a number from 1 to 5. Nearer to 1 indicates that you feel this statement to be *false or incorrect* and nearer to 5 indicates that you feel it is *more likely to be true*.

I like planning

Planning gives me a direction

I enjoy setting goals and working towards them

I like my work to have a focus

I never drift off topic

Other people have mentioned how sharp and focussed my writing is

Sometimes I set myself deadlines

I am clear about what I am trying to achieve

When I reach a certain end, I feel satisfied

I like to celebrate my success

Now add up your score and see what it says about you.

Result

35–50   You are probably a very organized worker. You have learned the power of setting goals in a way that allows you to focus on the outcome. Working to goals does not suit everyone but it certainly is a way to get things done and you understand and work well with that. You also like to celebrate or take time out to feel good about your success. That will give you a sense of self-worth. Read through the chapter to find out whether there are any other techniques that might just help you further.

20–34   You may find that there are times when you can plan easily and be totally focussed and other times when you cannot. You need to think about how useful planning techniques are to you and your work. Some people find them very helpful, but other people feel that they encroach on their creativity. However, being clear about for whom you are writing and what you want the reader to do can not only enable your work to be sharp but also save you time, as you will have to make fewer rewrites.

Below 20 Do you like to feel creative and free? Do you prefer to feel unhampered by structure and timescales? Even if you do, your work is bound to have some form of deadline or finishing point. Some people feel that writing should be timeless and free, and that is all well and good, but the longer you spend writing, the less time there is for the reader to access the message and take action. For example, if you take a week to polish off some advertising copy, that is one week of lost sales. Keep free writing as a hobby and start getting focussed now – and get that copy out!

It is so easy to allow ourselves to drift with our writing; after all, writing can be sheer pleasure and many writers will tell you that they enjoy playing with words. That is great for writing your memoirs or a story to entrance readers, but every hour you spend playing with the words is an hour lost on engaging with readers and possibly making sales (if that is your goal). Learning techniques to help you focus can make your writing sharper and increase your output (and that could increase your business) *and* allow you more time to do the things you want (such as drink coffee at the machine or chat with friends). So what are we waiting for? Let's get busy...

Remember this

For one week keep a log of the writing you do and how long it takes for each piece of writing to be completed. For example, if you write a letter, but then decide to write it again an hour later, include both times; if you look at a piece of writing but procrastinate, count up that time too. How long are you taking writing these letters, emails and reports? Would you be interested in reducing that?

Can you have too much time?

The short answer is yes! It is a strange phenomenon that, in life, jobs expand to fit the time available. For example, you will not find many people who have retired and wonder what to do all day. Most people will tell you that they don't know where they actually fitted a job into their day! The truth is that, if we have an hour to do the shopping in, we will get it done in an hour and if we have two hours then strangely it will take two hours.

What does this actually mean for us? It means that, if we are left to drift, there is every possibility that we will not be smart with our time – and remember, every hour that you are fiddling with words is an hour that your message is not reaching out to people.

Yes, time can be a strange continuum indeed. Under pressure and up against the clock, you may feel so hassled that you cannot think straight, but also, with too much time ahead of you, you may feel insufficient pressure and therefore achieve very little. So is there an optimum amount of pressure? Well there is, but it is not the same for everyone or in every situation and therefore I cannot be prescriptive.

Try it now

Think about the last piece of writing that you undertook. How did you manage your time in relation to it? Did you limit yourself or deliberately put yourself under pressure? Or did you feel that an investment in time was more appropriate?

There is also the issue of the level of importance. Sometimes we feel that something important should warrant more of our time and this is not always the most effective way of working. For example the famous writer Samuel Johnson wrote *Rasselas* in one week to pay for his mother's funeral. Many argue that it is possibly his finest work and yet his motivation was surely financial. If something is important – for whatever reason – we are motivated to get it done. Motivation can move mountains. What is your motivation for achieving your task?

Remember this

Taking a long time does not automatically ensure better results any more than being speedy and concise means that the job has been only half done.

Understanding your reader

OK, to be focussed (whether we have one hour or one week) necessitates that we need to know what we are doing and where we are aiming. For this we need to know the reader. Now I know that you cannot know every reader of every document but you can envisage where your document is heading and what it will be for. For example:

What	Advertising flyer for a Pizza outlet	Report for Head of Sales
Substance	One-page flyer	20-page document
Distribution	Homes throughout Anytown	Given to Head of Sales
Readership	Target of 30,000 people	Four people: Company Director and probably three others in sales
Best hopes	That the document will be retained	That the Head of Sales will feel I have done a good job

In the illustration above you will see that we have two completely different sets of target readers. In the first example, the pizza outlet, the typical reader will be at home. They will instantly make a decision about pizza (and if they don't eat pizza at all, they will discard the flyer immediately, no matter how well it is written). You might have thought that the very best hope was that the person receiving the flyer would order immediately (and indeed they may) but, thinking in the long term, I believe the best hope would be that the householder retains the leaflet and keeps it handy for when they next want to treat themselves. So many of these leaflets come through our letterbox, it is a tall order just to get someone to read them, let alone consider them worth keeping.

In this situation the writer will want to:

▶ engage the reader quickly

▶ create something memorable – perhaps an offer

▶ explain the product quickly

▶ use colour and images

▶ tell the reader what to do next.

In our second example the writer is creating a 20-page document for the Head of Sales. Our best hope here is that the document is distributed to key people such as the Director, who could be impressed by either the writing style or the ideas it contains. The document will be retained anyway because it will be an important report for the business and there may be some decisions made because of it.

In this situation the writer will want to:

► outline the issue succinctly

► present a clean, clear structure and writing within an accepted format

► engage and explain (using a business language style)

► create a professional image

► advise or recommend to the reader what to do next.

There is no way that you would write the same type of persuasive copy for an advert as for a business report. The readership is completely different and our hopes for the copy are also different.

Remember this

You need to relate this idea to your own copy or the product that you want to concentrate on. Who are your readership? What about others who might read the copy? We need to consider them too.

Now the next step: what does your reader want?

In our pizza example, the reader may not want a pizza right now but everyone eats food at some time and so the person who might be interested in this flyer may be:

► curious about what is being offered here

► hungry right now

► intrigued by an offer

► interested to know who and what company has moved into their area.

In the business report example, the reader may instead be:

- highly interested in the detailed content
- keen to look at pricing structures
- interested to see whether you have come up with any unique solutions
- testing you on your report writing skills.

In other words your readers will vary in their needs and desires and it is incorporating those into your work that will result in good-quality copy.

Key idea

Knowing your reader is highly important for you to be able to create the right copy that is pitched perfectly. Even if you don't actually know the reader personally, you can make an educated guess about what they want and need.

Some time for research

Finding out about your reader needs investment time. Think you don't have that time? Then think about the cost of getting it wrong.

In the pizza scenario above, if you had not had time to find out about your readers and what they want then you could have pitched your advertisement at completely the wrong level and the leaflets would have ended up in the waste bin. 'Okay,' you say, 'but I wanted to get them out quickly and I can always get some more done, it is only the cost of the printing that is lost.' I'm afraid that actually it is a lot more than that. The printing may have cost you £150 but, if you were planning to deliver them to the 25,000 homes in Anytown and you guessed that each home might have purchased an £8 pizza, that equates to a potential loss of £200,000, and that is not even considering that some homes will order two pizzas, side orders, or the future repeat business.

You see that the mistake of rushing your most important marketing document could cost you dear, not just now but also into the future. Combine a mistake like this with a very memorable name, for example, Monkey Pizzas, and, every time your customers see that name, the advert will hit the bin – they will not even look at the offer. This is marketing gone badly wrong and it is difficult to recover public interest once it is lost. How much better to have invested more time in the first instance.

Now let's consider the business report example. Hopefully you know the Head of Sales or at least how that person likes their reports presented. Presenting data in a comfortable format is a well-used persuasive ploy because as the reader recognizes the familiar format they relax and become more open to your suggestions. In other words they are lulled into a (maybe false) sense of security. Giving them a business report in a format very different from the one they usually use can make a bold statement but it can also create suspicion and can provoke a reaction such as 'This is different! Is the report any good?' One thing we don't want to do in persuasive writing is upset the reader.

The added concern with the business report is that it will be passed to other people who also have their own ideas. In other words you are trying to please not just one customer but several and they all have their way of doing things and their own agendas.

So, how do you build in some research?

Pizza delivery	Business report
Find out who else is in the area and what their advertisements look like	Make the secretary or PA your best friend and ask them what format of report is most acceptable
Find out what other pizza companies are charging and the details of any deals	Ask anyone who knows any of the potential readers to give you a run-down on what they are like, so that you can judge style
Undertake a house-to-house enquiry: how many pizzas do they buy? What are their favourite flavours?	Make sure you know about current policies and key areas of business so that you can make reference to them in your report
Order some pizzas from a rival business. How efficient were they? How fast did they come? How good was their customer service?	Have a look at a successful report and note the layout and style (including the language)

Key idea

Some of this research is around the product and some around the reader. You need to do both to increase your chance of hitting a 'bull's-eye'. Remember, this is time **invested**. Doing your research will really pay off when you see the response you get.

Setting goals and deadlines

Done the research? Now I expect you will want to set about creating great writing or copy, but before we go down that route we need to consider how we are going to organize our time and ensure the job is finished. In the most part, if you do not complete the job, you may as well have never started it. If you have no end product to show for your efforts, then the time you have spent on research and starting the project is wasted. We need to set some realistic goals and deadlines to make sure that you complete your copy on time.

Setting goals and deadlines has two functions:

▶ they enable you to plan your work and

▶ they guarantee you a path to meet your deadline and thereby hold the promise of fulfilment.

Not all projects come to fruition. Think about all the projects that you have started but have not completed. If you are like most people then I expect that over the years there have been quite a few and some of us will have a greater number than others. As you reflect, you may wonder why they did not happen. What went wrong? Well, maybe it was because:

▶ you did not know quite what you had to do

▶ someone 'moved the goal posts' and changed the project

▶ you did not get buy-in from the team

▶ you did not really think that you could do it

▶ you could not get going on the task

▶ the finishing post seemed so far in the distance that you did not bother.

All of these are very common reasons why we fail to complete tasks and totally justifiable. However, the fact is that we have not completed that piece of work, and therefore any time invested in it up until the stage when the project is discontinued is essentially wasted. Also, when we don't complete a task it sets off a little gremlin in our brains that registers the situation and we don't tend to forget these mishaps, mainly because we feel annoyed with ourselves deep in our subconscious. That is wasted energy and we can't afford too much wasted energy because we need all our energy to achieve the things we do want to do in life.

As persuasive writers we want to become achievers and this is where goal setting for the completion of writing projects can be useful.

I am sure that you may have heard of the mnemonic **SMART** used to describe goals. This means that they must be:

▶ **S** – specific

▶ **M** – measurable

▶ **A** – agreed

▶ **R** – realistic

▶ **T** – timed.

SMART goals need to include all of these elements. Let's look at what these statements indicate is missing:

▶ you did not know quite what you had to do (**it was not specific enough**)

▶ someone 'moved the goal posts' and changed the project (**it was not sufficiently measurable**)

▶ you did not get buy-in from the team (**they did not agree to it and therefore did not feel motivated to make it happen**)

▶ you did not really think that you could do it (**it did not seem realistic**)

▶ you could not get going on the task (**perhaps it was not achievable or realistic?**)

▶ the finishing post seemed so far in the distance that you did not bother (**the timing was at fault**).

Whereas we cannot say that, had these things been present, then the project would have been completed, we can certainly show that, where they were not present, it had a profound effect.

In fact a SMART element lies behind the reason for each of these excuses in the list of why a project has not been completed. Therefore having SMART goals set at the outset might have helped to pick up any of these problems *before* you started and could have saved you so much time and wasted energy.

Goals can help us to focus our work but they have to be sufficiently SMART to enable us to progress with the work. Where elements are lacking, it leaves the goal weak and the result is that it is less likely to succeed.

Remember this

Think about a project that you are working on right now. Test it against the SMART mnemonic and see if there are any areas of weakness. If there are, how can you reduce that weakness? Can you introduce the missing element?

Creating a deadline for yourself is simply good practice. Even when a project extends well into the future it is helpful to see an end to it and to know that every action on the way takes you one step nearer to completion. Break up your project into parts and give each a separate deadline, so that you can easily see progress and advancement.

Key idea

If meeting deadlines is a bit of a challenge for you, set one earlier than the real deadline and that way you have built some time in to overrun or recheck your work.

Write tight

Planning is good but now we are moving forwards towards your actual writing. Every section in this chapter is geared towards helping you write fast and with the minimum of wasted energy. It is all about getting it right first time as much as possible, because rewrites are good but take more of your precious time and you don't want to waste that; if anything, you want to be using your energy to write your next piece of persuasive text.

Keep the focus in mind at all times and consider your endgame – what *exactly* do you want the reader to do? You can do all the cajoling you want but at some point you need the reader to take action, otherwise your words are just that, words that were pleasant enough to read but meaningless.

Also remember what I said earlier: we need to assume that your reader will want to take action, otherwise they would not have read this far into your text. You are not trying to bamboozle anyone; in most instances you will just be providing the nudge that a good friend will give to another when they know that you secretly want to buy that item.

To craft an ending that assumes that the reader will want to take the next step, you could end with:

> **If you would like to order this please click below and you will be taken to the shopping cart.**

However, this is not very dynamic or tight and the mention of a shopping cart sounds like another set of pages of information that they will need to complete before they can access their goods. If you have previously whipped your customer into a frenzy of desire for the product or the customer is in a hurry, this will sound deflating and they might be put off. It also does not really provide the nudge we need. By rewriting we can change the line to:

> **Click on the button below to have your copy delivered straight into your mailbox RIGHT NOW.**

This is an improvement. It is enthusiastic and positive and will provide that nudge if the reader is indeed interested. Notice that it starts with a command (Click on the button) that assumes that the reader will do just that and the addition of RIGHT NOW screams immediacy.

It is good but it can still be tighter so let's look at that example again:

> **Click on the button below to have your copy delivered straight into your mailbox RIGHT NOW.**

By focussing on what we actually want the reader to do, and therefore tightening the suggestion, we can tighten this to:

Click HERE to have your copy NOW!

Notice how this shortened form is tighter and looks more exciting. Even the exclamation mark at the end makes it look more immediate and, if it was placed in a website advert for something I was interested in, I would click immediately.

Remember this

Copy with a punch means no wasted words or wasted time and so helps when working to a tight deadline. Eliminate any superfluous words and cut to the chase. Add only punctuation that enhances the message.

Celebrating your success

Celebrating your success is hugely important to do every time you make the effort to complete some great copy. You need to take some time out to congratulate yourself on putting in real effort and crafting persuasive prose that would impress anyone.

You may feel that celebrating is a bit silly because:

▶ this is your job anyway

▶ it is only a piece of writing

▶ you should not bother to get all excited about something that will be old news in an hour's time

or any of the other millions of similar reasons, but the truth is that you are now:

▶ thinking about your writing being more persuasive in its content

▶ keeping on track

▶ being highly focussed

▶ being highly organized

▶ creating copy that stimulates action.

How much more successful do you want to be? These are all highly valuable skills that would impress any company, and you are already creating copy and thinking this way, now.

Take time out to pat yourself on the back and tell yourself that it has been a good job, well done. Not only will you feel a million dollars but you will be automatically excited about tackling the next project. You have created your own instant motivation and that will stimulate you to push forward with your next project.

Remember this

When you have worked hard to launch any copy over which you have spent time, you must consider formally closing with a celebration, however small. Taking time out to celebrate will show you how far you have come and will formally 'launch' your copy or report to the customer.

Focus points

Even if it is not your usual style, accept the wisdom of structuring your work into sections, each one with a goal and a deadline. Chunk up large writing projects into smaller sections, each with their own goal.

Make sure you know exactly whom you are aiming your writing at. Who is your prime audience? What do you know or can guess? Who else might be involved?

Do your research. What will the reader be looking for? What will capture their attention?

Create goals and deadlines that help you structure your work and achieve it within the given time constraints. Ensure the job is achievable before you start and be realistic with your time – be SMART!

Don't forget to celebrate when you make it to the finishing line. Not only have you achieved something, and therefore deserve a reward, but celebrating will also mean that you are more likely to set goals and plan another writing triumph in the future.

Case studies

How does the setting of goals and identifying an endgame affect Leonie and Paul? Let's find out.

Although Leonie has written out all her details she realizes it is time to take a different approach. She knows that all her previous work (researching the company and looking again at her CV) makes good reference material and so she does not consider it wasted. It will just become notes for her next draft. Leonie considers her endgame to be a job at Sullivans; however, she recognizes that she may not have been paying enough attention to identifying and writing for her audience. She realizes that she does not know much about the human resources officer but decides to do a little further research. While looking on the website for Sullivans she sees that they have a competency framework showing behaviours and values that the company values in its staff. She makes a note of them as she is sure these are the ones that her application will be measured against. She plans to put the following day aside to rewrite her CV and create a profile that ties in with these qualities. The more she invests her time in this, the more she realizes that she really does want to work for this company. Leonie closes her eyes and imagines working there and she realizes that this is exactly the sort of career she wants. It is therefore really important that she go through her application again to ensure it sells her talents and shows her to her best advantage.

Paul has decided that Pan Haulage needs an advertising campaign but before he suggests it to Mr Pan he feels that he should plan all the details in advance and have a proper strategy, so that he can pitch the idea properly. He is willing to put in some extra time to plan this as he believes that planning *how* he pitches this idea is as important as the idea itself. He has to think about two customers: Mr Pan and what he wants; and the customers to the service and what they want. He reasons that Mr Pan wants to grow the business, but in a staged and measured way (no big or flash ideas, no international deliveries). To fulfil this, Paul decides that expanding the local business element of Pan Haulage might be the best way to go forward initially as it sounds fairly low risk. He decides to do some research locally to find out who uses delivery services and why they choose certain firms. From this research Paul hopes to create a package that is attractive to local business but at the same time allows

Pan Haulage to grow. Now that he has his endgame, he starts to plan some advertising copy and sets some goals for its completion. He knows that he will have to tread carefully, as the Pan family feel uncomfortable about change.

Next step

Hopefully, now that you have worked through this chapter you will acknowledge that, whether your persuasive copy is large or small, it is really helpful to be very clear about your endgame and also plan the way to reach it. It is equally important to celebrate your completion of goals, which can be at any level. Sometimes a cup of frothy coffee is enough, but preserving your own motivation will ensure that you repeat the process in the future. In the following chapter we will be looking at how we can move our research forward and increase our levels of success simply through active listening.

4

Techniques that Work

Goal – to enable the writer to become familiar with a range of persuasive writing techniques.

Diagnostic test

Answer each question by choosing a number from 1 to 5. Nearer to 1 indicates that you feel this statement to be *false or incorrect* and nearer to 5 indicates that you feel it is *more likely to be true*.

I understand that there are certain techniques I can use to increase my chances of being persuasive

The more I can rewrite my work, the sharper it will be

I think that people want to know the benefits of what I am proposing

I believe that people buy emotionally

I am always open to offers that friends have recommended

I am open to temptation if the offer is a good one

I like listening to stories

I believe you can describe something simply without being patronizing

I believe that if you are able to minimize the risk for people, that is a good and helpful thing to do

I like to keep the best offers for my friends

Now add up your score and see what it says about you.

Result

35–50   This chapter is for you! You are well aware that there are certain techniques that can help anyone to sharpen their writing and get the message across. You are right in that readers these days expect to be given an offer or the first chance at something you think will help them. People buy emotionally and need to solve problems both in their own lives and at work. You are confident that you can help these people; so read through the techniques given in this chapter and see how they fit with your own style and the way you like to communicate.

20–34   You may have felt less certain about the statements on the previous page. When you read through this chapter you will not only feel clearer about the Diagnostic test but also see how each section can help you. These techniques are used by many writers of persuasive copy and some writers will use more than one in a single document. What we are looking at here is human behaviour and how people react. If we can incorporate that into our work, it will automatically become more persuasive.

Below 20 Your lower score here indicates that you are not completely happy with most of these comments. Have a look through again and see whether it was just a few that you feel uncomfortable with, or whether there is a lot more. Writing persuasively means writing with a view to persuading the other person to take action in some way. To enable that to happen we have to present the copy in a way that links to human behaviour. Read through the chapter and then try the Diagnostic test again. You may find that you are actually already doing some of these things without recognizing them as techniques.

First, let's get the mystery of the magic wand out of the way. There is no one way to persuade everyone. If only I had that to offer you, I would be making millions, but I am afraid that it is right up there with the fountain of youth. However, what we do have are a number of techniques that are known to be persuasive either used on their own or in conjunction with other techniques.

These techniques will make your message more accessible and therefore easier to take on board. They will soften resistance and present your text or material in a more persuasive way.

Remember this

Open a magazine or look at some advertising copy for something that you want. Why do you want it? Is it the item or the way it is described? Is it a lifestyle or does it cause your emotions to fluctuate? Whatever you are experiencing is what others will experience too. Readers are just like you and me and a proportion of us will want those same things.

Selling the benefits

When we buy into an idea or decide to purchase an item, we do so for a number of reasons and one of those is that we feel that, in some way, our lives will be the better for having it. This relates to whether you are buying a new house or the subscription to a lifestyle magazine, for example:

Benefits to buying a new house	Benefits to buying a lifestyle magazine subscription
My friends will admire me; the house will say something about me	Carrying it demonstrates to people who I am, my style and my life
I will have my own space that can represent me (and there may be more space for *my* things)	As a subscriber I am now in an elite club: I receive my magazine a day earlier than it is in the shops and have access to special offers
I will appear solid and dependable, a pillar of the community	I will look trendy and people will assume my life is like that in the magazine

There may be additional benefits that you can think of. However, many copywriters will miss the main point here and that is why you will see advertisements such as:

House for Sale

Terrace house, two bedrooms one bathroom, built in 1987. Please ring XXXXX.

This is very typical of a descriptive advertisement. It says what it is but it does not entice us with a lifestyle or personal image, like the examples above. In other words it does not sell itself to us. It could give us just a taste of how we would feel living there, rather than simply the basics. We could instead show the reader how living here would enhance their lifestyle and say so much more about them, for example:

House for Sale

Be the envy of your friends and hold great parties in this stylish two bedroom terrace house. Ring XXXXX.

This second advert may have cost you a little more (if you were paying by the word) but I would be willing to bet that you will receive a much greater response, because you have presented some of the benefits of choosing this house and you have tapped into the reader's real wants. They don't just want a house, they want a lifestyle.

Similarly, a magazine subscription that simply asks you to buy is unlikely to reap many responses, but one that includes strap lines such as:

> Let people know who you are
>
> Be seen with the best
>
> Let other people make their own assumptions

is more likely to be successful. In essence you are telling people that if they want to join your 'club' and be in with the 'in' crowd then this is one route they can take quickly and easily.

Try it now

Think about any recent copy you have written. Go through it again and look at whether you have simply described the product, or spelled out the benefits (including the emotional ones). What could you have written?

Emotionally speaking

When we buy we may be thinking logically but actually we are acting emotionally. Certain images can conjure up strong emotions in us, some of which appeal only to one stratum of society; for example, not everyone loves the countryside and therefore a campaign focussed on country living would not suit everyone. However, there are others that are more general, for example the notion of home and family.

Remember this

If I said to you 'and then he turned up in his gleaming red Ferrari' what images and emotions would that stir in you: desire? Greed? Strength? The wind rush of speed? Do you think: money, style, romance?

In this short statement I have managed to stir up ideas and emotions that you have wholly conjured yourself and that carry you into another world – which is why writers use such images.

Emotions allow us to tap into people at a deeper level. If I offered you a vitamin pill and said, 'Take it – it's good for you', you would feel less than inspired and you might even refuse. However, if I said, 'Take it – it will make you feel really good', you would be more likely to take it, because I am tapping into your emotions and feelings and you already know how wonderful it is to feel really good.

Look at this question:

> Do you remember your first real bike?

How does that make you feel? What emotions does that question evoke in you? For some people these may be unhappy emotions – perhaps you fell off and hurt yourself (remember you will not always get a 100 per cent hit rate) – but for many it will stimulate emotions of joy, achievement, freedom and excitement.

Capture emotions and embed them into your copy, especially if it is sales copy, and see how people immediately identify with your ideas. Write emotionally to stimulate the senses and create energy. Ask your readers 'Do you want to feel great? Do you want to feel amazing?' because they will identify with those feelings and want to recapture them.

Key idea

Think about images and iconic situations such as a traditional Christmas or Fourth of July celebrations; what feelings to they evoke? Create the emotion with words and then prune relentlessly until you are left with your final copy.

Some copy actually targets specific emotions such as greed or guilt (think of chocolate advertising), as the persuasive writer knows that we are all subject to these feelings. For example:

> *Greed* – 'Go on, you know you want to. No one's looking, you can just take it and add it to your collection and no one will know except you. One more won't hurt. Go on, go on...'

Guilt – 'You know you shouldn't have but it was just so tempting. Trouble is that, now you have done this, you must do that too...'

Envy – 'Everyone else has one of these and, if you have one, you really will be in with the "in crowd"...'

Recommendations

Nothing is better than a personal recommendation. After all, if your friend has said that you need it, then you probably do. It is for this reason that catalogue companies are very generous to customers who are willing to send them the names of their friends who they feel might also benefit from this awesome offer.

Celebrity endorsements are also a form of recommendation. You buy something because you believe that your favourite celebrity has told you to. They have told you that it is the greatest thing ever and that they always use one – and so should you. Real fans cannot help purchasing whatever their favourite celebrity is selling because it is yet another way of feeling closer to their idol. After all, you may not be them, or even with them, but you can use their products and be like them.

You might think that this idea is limited to advertising but not so; even businesses can be persuaded by the knowledge that others recommend the product. For example, if you were selling office space you might just let it be known that you have another large and prestigious company moving in next week. This will stimulate people to think: 'If it's good enough for that company then we want to be there too.' Anyone offering office space or industrial offices will tell you that, if they can just get one well-known company in, the others will follow. In other words, the others will follow because they will have the endorsement of great neighbours.

Key idea

Recommendations ask the buyer to show trust: trust that we are telling the truth about the product or service, and trust that the person providing the recommendation really does use the product. When it comes together, personal recommendation can be an excellent form of persuasion.

Repetition

Location, location, location.

I came. I saw. I conquered.

A government of the people, by the people, for the people.

Why do things look better in threes? I'm afraid I really don't know the answer to this, but the rule is that people love threes! The power of threes has been recognized for many a long time as a significant way of delivering impact and many passages in holy books are written incorporating threes.

You can use the power of three in a subtle way:

Feeling lost? Lonely? Inconsolable?

Or even a more funky way:

do it, Do It, DO IT!

It still has impact and the easy repetition ensures your message is memorable.

Writing in threes is a form of repetition, and repetition can become slightly hypnotic. In his famous 'I have a dream' speech Martin Luther King mentioned:

- ▶ 'One hundred years later' four times
- ▶ 'Now is the time' four times
- ▶ 'We cannot/we can never' five times
- ▶ 'Go back to' six times
- ▶ 'I have a dream' seven times
- ▶ 'Let freedom ring' nine times.

He had a message to get across and his speech was crafted to ensure that it had maximum impact and lodged in the memory. Today it is acknowledged as one of the finest speeches of all time.

Key idea

Repetition can be used hypnotically to calm the mind and reinforce ideas, or firmly to punch home key messages. Repetition is hypnotic – 'You are feeling sleepy, you are feeling sleepy, sleep, sleep...' – and as such is very comforting. (Notice how children love the same story to go to sleep to, read over and over again. It makes them feel safe).

Next time you look at some impressive copy, note how much repetition is involved and whether you believe this makes a difference to your level of interest.

Solve the problem

Readers want their problems solved and everyone has problems. This simple point can make a huge difference to the number of people who read your advertising. For example, imagine that you have just invented a cream that aids baldness and helps hair to grow. Advertising it as:

A new cream for baldness

(which is descriptively correct) will have some impact but not as much as if you had advertised it as:

Immediate hair growth

or

Fantastic hair, instantly

because these are the solutions that your readers are looking for.

Remember this

Copy with a punch means no wasted words and working to a tight deadline. Eliminate any superfluous words and cut to the chase. Add only punctuation that enhances the message. Concentrate on what the reader wants – the solution – and focus on that.

Collaborating with the reader

We all like to feel involved, and none more so than the reader. As writers, when we collaborate with the reader we allow them to feel part of our world. We can tell them 'secrets' that to the reader feel like intimate insights into our life, when in fact we are actually inviting everyone in.

This technique is used by writers of the real life columns that appear in every newspaper. They tell you things about their world and then ask you not to tell anyone. Considering their paper has gone out to millions of readers, this hardly counts as a secret, but we feel special because they have put their trust in us.

From gaining the readers' collaboration it is only one short step to making them our friends and thereby creating an open market for recommendations to various products or endorsements.

Try it now

Look out for a column like this in your regular reading copy (a newspaper or magazine). There is bound to be a personal life column in there somewhere, even if it is featured on only one day. Look at how the writer draws the reader into their life, asking you questions such as 'Well would you?', as if your opinion matters to them, attempting to create a rapport with the reader. Check how many techniques you can find and how often they are repeated.

Bizarrely, reading about the problems of others makes us, as readers, feel much better. When writers write a column about their difficult life they are often manipulating the reader to feel better about their own lives and that is why they are such popular reads.

Remember this

Don't be afraid to allow your writing style to come through. People are persuaded by people they like, so display your personality through your writing and you will appear more real to the reader.

Further techniques that can make a humungous difference

BE POSITIVE

What is wrong with this?

> To be honest about 50% of the time your work is below par. You seem to rush things and your copy is sloppy and not up to the required standard. I would like you to inform me as to how you are going to rectify this situation.

Full marks if you think it was somewhat negative; also, did you feel told off? It felt like a dressing down by the head teacher to me and that is something to bring out the worst in anyone! I think that if I went into a meeting with this person they would be on the attack and I would probably be very defensive.

The point is that from this prose we can see that, although 50 per cent of the work is 'below par' the other 50 per cent of the work must be anywhere on the scale of good to great – but why is this not mentioned? Surely if you want someone to change it is not a good idea to get them so fed up with you that they give up or plot some revenge.

Let's have a go at writing that same paragraph more positively:

> So far I have been really pleased with most of your work. On the whole I feel that you have mastered the way we like to do things in this organization, but, as in all things in life, we like staff to continue to strive for improvement. For example, I have noticed that you are often very busy and I thought we could meet to chat through the impact of that and discuss some possible solutions.

Isn't that more likely to encourage someone to come to the meeting and be more receptive to ideas?

Remember this

Use positivity in your copy to encourage the reader. When they feel good about themselves, they will feel good about the product or message too.

ENCOURAGING A YES RESPONSE

Telesales people use this technique all the time. They ask you a number of questions to which the answer is highly likely to be 'Yes' in the hope that you will continue with this pattern because it has become automatic. For example:

Operator	Respondent
Are you having a good day today?	Yes
Can I ask you a few questions?	Yes
Your account with us has been going for some time now hasn't it?	Yes
Can I just take a moment to tell you about a new product we are launching for people just like you?	Yes... errr

Ever felt caught in this one? You have actually invited the caller to tell you about the product they are trying to sell you. You could slam the phone down but most of us would not do that; most of us would politely listen – after all, we didn't say no when we had the chance, did we?

This is a common technique that we can consider for our writing, only in our case we are getting the reader to think 'Yes' rather than actually say it.

> **Would you like the latest XYZ****?**
>
> **Would you like it today?**
>
> **Would you like it right now?**
>
> **Turn the page and I will tell you how that can be in your hands by 4.00 p.m. today.**

Would you turn the page? I would!

This uses a number of techniques together: excitement, threes, yes questions and so forth.

Another derivative of this techniques is to ask the reader a question that makes it look odd if they say no; for example:

> **If I could tell you a way of making £500 in five minutes, would you be interested?**

or

> **If there was an easy way to lose weight would you want it?**

This technique is used by many sales personnel because they know that we are programmed to be honest and curious and would find it difficult to answer no to these questions.

METAPHORS, STORIES AND SIMILES

There are other ways of getting our message across rather than just being direct. Telling a story can make our message more acceptable and the notion that the reader has figured out the connection for themselves encourages the reader to feel clever and knowledgeable. For example:

> **I would never blame you for being cautious about signing up today but I must just tell you a story about one of my other customers who did not sign up. He was buying...**

This would be followed by a story of woe that would make the listener (or reader) empathize with the person who did not sign up and make them think 'My goodness, that could be me.' When the storyteller now tells you that, if you do sign up, you can cancel at any time in the next seven days, you will be more inclined to do so. The power of stories and metaphors lies in the fact that, in the days before people could read, they were a powerful method of warning children of the dangers in life. They are a very strong part of our heritage and we tend to be drawn in by them.

Metaphors and similes are also great because they paint a picture for us in our minds. When we write 'Ever felt like a used sock?', the reader knows exactly what we are describing and the image it conveys is far more persuasive than a description of that feeling can ever be.

Many writers of persuasive copy will use this three-pronged approach:

▶ present the initial hook and get their attention

▶ wander off into a story, and then

▶ return to the sales message.

This is not actually dissimilar to how we converse. However, the point here is that the story is not just any story; it is one that has a prime message for the reader and prepares them to accept your main sales message. A good example of this is price.

If I told you that my magic beans were £250 each you might wince and say no thanks, but if I:

- told you about the beans (how much would owning your own magic bean mean to you?) **Once only offer – magic bean – there is only one! – you have stumbled on a hidden secret** (ummmm, sounds interesting and arouses curiosity...)

- progressed into a story about how several people I had met wanted to buy a bean off me and offered me at first £1,000 and then more and more until the offer was over £10,000 for a bean, but I refused because I wanted it to go to someone who would benefit from its properties, someone honourable and good

- then offered you the bean for £250

suddenly the price seems more acceptable, and of course the person has recognized that I am the right person (honourable and good) to take charge of such a bean. I could almost convince myself that it is destiny and the bean chose me!

We are more committed to conclusions that we have drawn for ourselves than to what we are told. If you had told me that the bean had chosen me I would not have believed it, but, because I worked it out myself, it makes perfect sense.

VALUES AND PERCEPTIONS

While we are on the subject of magic beans, how do you feel about the £250? How much should a magic bean cost, anyway? The answer is that there is no set price for magic beans and they cost (like many things) however much someone will pay for them.

If we perceive that this bean will change our lives for the better, then £250 is probably very cheap; throw in a few extra wishes and it becomes a bargain. In the example above it is really our perception that is setting the price and as persuasive writers we are in a prime position to shape that perception. There is often no set value to any product or service – just perception.

BEING CONSISTENT

In the same way that we might encourage a line of 'Yes' answers, consistency is something that the reader feels comfortable with.

We also do not like cancelling and so, in the previous example, many people will not cancel the agreement. After all, if we agreed at the time, it would seem inconsistent if we suddenly cancelled. Most people don't like that feeling; it feels uncomfortable, as if we had not made a good enough decision in the first place – and we don't want to appear to be bad at making decisions. We don't like to change our minds and therefore in your writing you need to assure the reader that they have made the right decision. Keep people interested too, as it is easier to keep a customer than to find a new one.

A BIRD IN THE HAND

In an experiment children were seated in a classroom with some sweets in front of them. They were told that, if they did not eat the sweets, there would be more sweets for them later, but, if they ate the ones in front of them, they would have to forfeit the others. Most of the children could not wait and chose immediate gratification over long-term gain.

How many of us are still like that? Amazingly many of us are and, for that reason, offering something right now can tempt the reader to indulge – even if it is something that they don't really want. For example:

> **Sign up today to receive our new catalogue.**

> **Ring through today and we will send you not only the catalogue but also this unique set of teaspoons.**

Anyone need extra teaspoons? Many people don't, but this type of persuasive text works very well and the phone lines are red hot because we can't resist an extra something that appears to be for nothing.

FOLLOWING THE HERD

How many times do we do what we do because everyone else is doing it? Ever bought into the 'latest' haircut or worn certain clothes or shoes? We do these things because we feel comfortable following what everyone else is doing. Creating a feeling of familiarity and 'part of the herd' is what ties us into trends and ensures that vast numbers of people all end up doing the same thing or buying the same product.

We fall for it all the time, especially in fashion, when we are told that hems are a certain length this year or that jackets are being worn this way or that. It is simply what persuades us to go out and buy new items when our wardrobes are already bursting with perfectly good clothes from last year's must-have collection. The fashion industry is a master of persuasion as it also creates the level of emotional desire necessary to enable us to part with large amounts of money for items that are of only passing relevance.

Look out for new trends and see how they can link to your own persuasive writing. There will always be themes and products that attract people, and, if people can buy into that by responding to you, then that is persuasive in itself. At the time of writing this book, recycling and green issues are very much in vogue. If you are able to point out the links between your proposal and these issues you may find it tips the balance in your favour.

MAKE IT SIMPLE FOR THE CUSTOMER

Remember the section on collaboration, where we were trying to get the customer to say yes? This is also a form of making it simple for the customer. If the customer has to think about anything in too much depth, they might just say no or decide not to bother. For this reason it is essential that, when you are persuading your reader, you focus on making the next step very easy for the reader. For example:

Simply text: 4 me to 99375

This makes it very simple for the customer to commit. If they have to fill out forms or call helplines that might be busy, they will pass on by and will be seduced by someone else's wares. Make it quick and easy to gather the data.

MINIMIZE THE RISK

Earlier I mentioned that someone could be persuaded further if they felt that they could cancel the deal, perhaps within the next seven days. What we are doing here is minimizing risk to the customer. As the reader is working their way through your text they will be thinking of aspects of their life where your ideas may not fit so well. I call these the 'Ah but' moments: when the reader may think 'Ah but it would not work in this situation.' As a writer you are not necessarily there to counter those arguments and so you need a way of ensuring any obstacle can be overcome. We do this by minimizing the risk to practically nothing. For example:

You can't lose with our 100% money back guarantee.

Do you feel that you can't lose? Many people would and therefore it becomes a persuasive offer. (In truth many people do not try to claim the money back, even if the goods do not live up to expectation – see Being consistent. They decide that it is just not worth the trouble or that they don't want to look foolish.)

Another example may be:

> **If you can show me that you have followed all my 'Steps to Success' and not recouped your investment within 28 days, I will pay you double the money you have spent – yes, double!**

To make such an offer the product surely has to be brilliant, doesn't it? Well very possibly it is; however, note that the writer has minimized your risk by offering you double your money *but* you will have to prove to them that you followed all the steps in the Steps to Success programme first and within 28 days. When the reader is buying, this seems like a wonderful offer, but 28 days is quite a tight timescale for people to complete a programme such as this and it would be easy to slip beyond the timeframe.

Often this technique is used as a sweetener to the reader to ensure that they feel not only safe but also good about the purchase. After all, if there is a 100 per cent money-back guarantee:

- the seller must feel confident about their product (they would not want loads of returns, would they?)

- I can get my money back easily and it is a bit like a 'no-brainer' – there is no risk at all to me

- therefore I am making a very well-informed and safe decision in choosing this product over the other one (with no guarantee)

- I know that I am a good decision maker!

See how risk minimization suddenly becomes an easy decision for the reader to make – and they feel good about doing it too.

Focus points

Techniques are there to be used. In fact we all use them every day without thinking about them.

Sell the benefits and make sure you provide solutions to people's problems. Everyone finds aspects of life difficult but, if you are offering a great solution, shouldn't everyone know about it?

Make all your writing positive, even if you are just responding to an email. You will be surprised at the improved reaction you get from the reader.

Create excitement about your offer; after all, if you are not excited, why should your reader be?

Make it simple for the customer to make the next move. One way of doing this is by offering them a very quick way of taking the next step. Another way is to remove the 'Ah but' reaction from the reader by minimizing the risk to almost nothing.

Case studies

Let's see how some of these techniques work out with Leonie and Paul.

Leonie looks at her profile page. It all seems a bit daunting now that she is set to design it and she realizes that she has to sell herself. She flicks back through the techniques and decides that there are some ideas she would like to try. She thinks that writing bulleted points in groups of three would work well and can think of some recommendations that she can use that are other than the ones given as references on her CV. She would also like to highlight some of the skills she has learned so that she is able to transmit her credibility and professionalism. She looks at the person specification to gauge what type of person they are looking for and also at the competence list she found on their website. She decides to make it easy for the reader by tying each paragraph in her profile to each point and gives examples where she can. She also wants to make it easy for the reader to contact her and decides to do this by enclosing a stamped and addresses envelope with her application. As a final point she reads over everything again, just to see whether there is anything she has missed. Phew! She has never put so much into an application before, but she really wants this job and feels a little more optimistic about her application this time.

Paul's research shows him that he is right: local people do not use Pan Haulage but would be more than willing to do so. For some reason they seem to have the perception that it is not a very efficient or organized business, just because it is a family firm. No one had any negative comments – just the feedback based on perception. Paul thinks that this is easier to turn around than a bad reputation and he knows that Pan Haulage runs very efficiently and effectively; he just needs to convince others of that. He thinks that he could write an advertorial for the local paper and also do some promotions work – but only if Mr Pan will let him. Paul is very excited by this idea but knows that he has to convince Mr Pan first. He thought about putting together a PowerPoint presentation at home but Mr Pan does not like technology and this may go against him. He therefore decided to present the data, not as he prefers, but as Mr Pan would like it: in a report with spreadsheets. He decides to pitch it not only to Mr Pan but to the whole family because he has noticed that both Mrs Pan and old Mr Pan both play a large part in the decision making. He has also decided to bring in the story of another company that suffered the same kind of misconceptions and managed to turn itself around. He is hoping that Mr Pan makes the connection. He has the data but wants the whole meeting to be focussed on the positive of what they can do – not what they are not doing now. He also has an idea about introducing a customer charter so that customers can see what they do and how they operate and the company can measure its success against it. He is excited to see what the Pans make of his ideas.

Next step

In this chapter we have covered a lot of different techniques. Some of them suit certain situations and others are more general. It is for you to read them all and put them into the context of your work. Some of the techniques can also be used together or in harmony. Play with the ideas and see how you can incorporate them in your work and how others use them in their work and advertising. In the following chapter we will be looking at persuasive language and how specific words can have leverage over the reader to encourage certain actions.

5

Persuasive Language

Goal – to become more familiar and practised with persuasive language.

Diagnostic test

Answer each question by choosing a number from 1 to 5. Nearer to 1 indicates that you feel this statement to be *false or incorrect* and nearer to 5 indicates that you feel it is *more likely to be true*.

I understand that persuasive language has to be crafted

Understanding the impact of my writing is a higher-level communication tool

I feel comfortable going back over my work and reanalysing it

I believe that the reader deserves good-quality, clear communication

I always need to find out as much as possible about my reader

I think that it is important to showcase good writing

I understand that starting with impact can grab the reader's attention

Sometimes simple messages are best

I like to think that I am crafting my writing for the reader and aim to be helpful

All writing can be improved

Now add up your score and see what it says about you.

Result

35–50   This score indicates that you are very aware of the impact of your writing. You are right to be so aware, as persuasive writing is an art that can be used in many different arenas. Already you will be thinking about your current style and how that can be improved. You will also be thinking about new market areas where you can use this skill to achieve great success. Today's market is highly competitive and that means that you need enhanced communication skills to stay ahead. This chapter will give you further insight into this highly desirable craft.

20–34   You may still be unsure that persuasive writing is for you. If that is the case then go back and skim-read the previous chapters. Perhaps you are worried that there is a lot to remember or feel daunted by the task of putting it all into operation. If this is the case, please do not worry. Later in the book we will be covering practical examples that will help to instil more confidence and show you ways to incorporate all that you learn into real situations.

Below 20   Your lower score here indicates that you are not completely happy with most of these comments. Perhaps you feel that persuasive writing should not be such hard work and that you did not foresee having to constantly revisit it and re-edit. Unfortunately, any enhanced skill needs work and dedication to master its complexity. Learning a skill can be a challenging path but is always one worth taking. If you are feeling a little challenged, please persevere, because I know that you can improve your persuasive writing skills with this book and that will have a huge payoff in your future life.

Writing is a wonderful thing. Can you remember a time when you were not able to read or write? Perhaps it was when you were very young and someone else read to you. It was so comforting, sitting on someone's knee or snuggling up close to a relative and hearing wonderful stories unfold. If you were sharing a book then maybe you would see those wonderful words that spidered across the page and thought them magical – after all, how could a few scribbles take you to such wonderful worlds of fantasy?

Remember this

Think back; do you remember learning to read? I mean the actual act of learning? If you do, what did it feel like? Was it exciting or daunting? Did you know that you were accessing a gate to a future of information?

Not many people can remember learning to read, but I want to take you back there so that you are able to appreciate what a tremendous thing reading and writing is. When you can read, you can access all manner of information and it will give you an understanding of all the phenomena in the world. When you can write, you are able to impact on the world, report what you see and find and share your opinions. But when you can write persuasively you are able to influence others to see the world your way and persuade them to take action, whether that be rallying for the defence of something or raising funds for your chosen charity.

Writing as a communication tool

Writing is a phenomenal communication tool – but not the only one.

Remember this

On a sheet of paper, take a moment to make a quick list of other communication tools that are used today.

On that list you could have any of the following:

▶ visual media (television, films, etc.)

▶ audio media (radio, sound systems, etc.)

▶ computers and the Internet

▶ paper-based methods (memos, letters, reports, etc.)

▶ body language and facial signals

▶ text language and symbols

▶ sign language

and probably many others!

This means that we communicate in a variety of ways and some methods may be more suited to certain situations than others. For example, you might find it unusual to receive the communication of a job offer in symbols, or to be asked to commit to buying a house by a televised link. In both those instances we tend to rely on more formal methods of communication such as written contracts and deviating from this would seem odd.

For this reason we need to select the most appropriate method or format for our situation to ensure that writing will be the most effective communication tool (and this is before we even think of switching on our persuasive writing techniques). It is only when we have selected the best form of communication that we can then look at the options within that form. For example, if we wanted to try to get our boss to increase the number of people in the team we could do that through a memo, a letter, an email, a report and so forth. Selecting the most appropriate format is very important, as that will be the first thing you will be judged on. If the method is inappropriate, then you have automatically reduced your chances of success, as the reader will have been distracted by the method before they even get as far as the message. For example, sending the director a text message may be so unacceptable that they balk at the cheek of it and may never even read the message. Not a good idea because I am sure that you remember that one of the techniques mentioned previously was to make it easy for the reader?

Key idea

Spend some investment time in considering the best method of communication. It could have an immediate impact on how your message is received.

The other side of writing

The other side of writing is reading.

Remember this

You are writing to relay a message to the reader – not because you think your words look great. However brilliant your prose, if the reader does not understand what you have written, or what you want them to do, you have failed to communicate effectively.

Therefore we must keep the reader in our focus at all times. To be persuasive we must not consider our egos; we should be firmly in touch with their egos instead.

Well, that is great if there is only one reader, but you might be thinking at this point 'How can I write for the reader when I need this communication to go out to hundreds (or thousands) of readers?' If you are writing for the Internet or advertising copy, then this may well be the case. It is rare to achieve a 100 per cent success rate when you have so many variables, but there are ways we can streamline our communication.

Your first port of call must be any market research or information on your readers. Like it or not, readers (or customers) do tend to fit into a 'type'. Market researchers use these types to categorize their main target group. They fall into five main types:

Innovators – these people buy journals and are highly open to new and innovative ideas. They are the gadget conscious and 'techies' of the marketplace and are willing to experiment with anything new. They can be highly influential but make up only 2 per cent of the market.

Adopters – these people are change agents. They take on new ideas if they feel that it will have a beneficial impact on their business or lifestyle. They will research thoroughly before making a purchase. They make up about 15 per cent of the market.

Early majority – these people are slower to enter the market and will only try things out after their peers have given it their approval. They care about the reputation of the product and are looking for a 'guarantee' if possible. They rely on mass media for information about what they need and represent about 39 per cent of the market.

Late majority – these people are thinking about buying when the innovators and adopters have moved on to something else. They wait for a fall in prices and assurance that the product has become the universally accepted solution. Cost is a big issue for them and they want value through additional aspects such as customer support. They represent another 39 per cent of the market.

Traditionalists – they will wait until they actually need the product or service. They may even buy things that other buyers will feel are obsolete in the belief that they have finally stood the test of time. They make up only 5 per cent of the market.

What if you come up with two ideas – for example, two differently worded texts – and you are not sure which one would be the more effective? You would not want to miss a whole readership by getting it wrong, would you? Suddenly your campaign seems high risk.

Fortunately there is a solution to this dilemma: the split test. In split testing, you set up two customer groups and market your text to each and see which one has the most success. For example, if you were not sure which website has the more appealing text you might set up two separate sites and then monitor them over a period of time to see which one has the more 'hits'. If you are writing an e-book there is nothing to stop you marketing your book under two different titles (as long as you make it clear to the customer and offer to refund the money if they already have the other book). This would at least give you an indication which is the more appealing advertisement, front cover or title.

Key idea

Start to think like the customer and you will get to know them better. Once you know them you can target your text more effectively.

Making assumptions

In the previous section we looked at how we can begin to think about our reader being in a certain category and now we are going to stretch that idea a little more.

To understand our market we have to make certain assumptions about our readers. I am sure many of you know the old adage about not making an assumption because it makes an

ASS out of U and ME – ASSUME

However, in persuasive writing we have to make assumptions because, although we may not hit the 100 per cent mark, we have to know that we are hitting more than if we had not made these assumptions. For example, if I decided to launch a new cookery book that focuses on cakes and baking, it is unlikely that I would get many sales from the local weight loss clinic. In fact I may decide that it is not even worth my time figuring out how to write persuasively to them because most people there would not buy the book (at least openly) because it is full of temptations that they do not need. I think that is a safe assumption based on the fact that most people attend a weight loss clinic to lose weight and my book is probably not helpful to them.

In the same way, you need to make assumptions about the readers you will be targeting.

Remember this

Look at the categories once again. They are listed below:

* Innovators
* Adopters
* Early majority
* Late majority
* Traditionalists

Note beside each what assumptions you can make about each group. Are they likely to have families? Do they fall into a certain income stream?

If we assume that all our readers are going to be individuals, and that you are truly writing for everyone individually, then you will have to make your writing very bland and it will not be so easy to target your persuasive words. If you dilute the entire message you will not transmit any message of worth. Our assumptions may later be proven to be incorrect for some people but we need to make them anyway to enable us to work with words.

The language we use

Now on to those words that we use. I hope that you would not write a book for ten-year-olds in the same way as you would for five-year-olds (or even adults). I would expect you to change your language accordingly so that the communication is effective. If a child puts the book down and does not read it, then the moment of communication is lost – and that is the same with your copy.

The language we use is incredibly rich and has developed to suit its purpose. It can be blunt and hard or exquisitely charming, it can reveal your inner feelings or convey whatever persona you wish. You can both hide behind language and also inadvertently reveal your true self through it.

Words have texture, depth and colour and through them you can weave material that can evoke emotions and create longing in your reader.

Look again at the five types of customer used in the previous exercise. To refresh your memory, they are:

► Innovators

► Adopters

► Early majority

► Late majority

► Traditionalists

Now consider that you are writing persuasive copy for items targeting these groups. What words would you use? What words do you think these types would react favourably to? (Fill them in above.) For example, Innovators would be attracted to words such as 'experimental', 'exclusive', 'new', 'novel' and 'innovative' whereas the Early majority may tune into 'tried', 'tested' and 'guarantee'.

Key idea

Start to think like a persuasive writer. What type of reader is your copy primarily aimed at? What do they like? What type of home do they have? What type of life do they have? Where do they shop? What do you think their aspirations are? What words do you think would attract them?

If you are unsure, don't forget that you can perform a split test to ascertain which method has the greatest impact.

Analysing the written word

When you write a novel, the editor will go through the manuscript and make various points regarding the characters, plot and prose. There then follows the agonising line edit whereby your masterpiece is analysed line by line, word by word. Each word has to earn its right to be in that sentence and each word has to be the most appropriate word for whatever the writer is attempting to convey. When there is conflict between the editor and writer, the writer needs to be able to justify why they used that particular word – there must be a reason.

Now that you are a persuasive writer, you need to go through this process by yourself. You may not have an editor to hand but you can go through each line and ask yourself these questions:

▶ Why did I use this particular word?

▶ Does it reach out to my readership?

▶ Will my readers know and understand what I need to convey?

▶ Will this writing convince my readers that they should take action?

Gather together some of your favourite advertisements or persuasive copy and study them. If you read a regular column in a magazine, look at that too, but this time with a critical eye. Why has the writer constructed it in the way they have? If there are 'pull quotes', why were those sentences particularly chosen? (Pull quotes are part of the written feature that are presented throughout the text in larger writing. They are there to tempt or persuade the reader to stop and read that particular feature and are usually chosen by the editor.) Would you have chosen different words?

Remember this

Words have great power. Arm yourself with a good-quality dictionary and a thesaurus (or find a good online equivalent). Make words your friends and they will reward you in becoming a highly valuable tool that will take you further in life.

Starting with impact

This is the most important section in this chapter.

When we look at the title of something, whether that is a book, a report or an advertising hoarding, we may be turned on or off instantly. If you are curious enough to read the text underneath, then that may again intrigue you sufficiently to finish the journey, or it may lead you to give up. Unfortunately, this all sounds a little wishy washy and high risk and we want more solid results. If you want to be persuasive you simply cannot afford to be casual about first impressions.

In writing, we talk about the 'hook'. That is the line, image or phrase that hooks the reader into exploring a little further. Some hooks are more forceful and the reader will instantly buy in or out, but others are more subtle. You need to decide which approach to take with each project, but, whichever it is, you cannot afford to miss out this very important step.

Who will be your competition? If you are designing a leaflet for another pizza delivery scheme in the neighbourhood, although the volume of people who would use this service is high, the likelihood that you have similar competition is quite high too and therefore you are in a highly competitive field. Your leaflet simply *must* stand out from the rest if it is even going to be picked up, let alone pinned on a 'must keep' board in the kitchen. If you are offering made-to-measure handbags starting at £2,000 each, there is less likely to be immediate competition but the volume of your customer base is much smaller too and so once again you need to be highly persuasive to engage people. In other words, it does not matter whether you are selling pizzas or expensive handbags; you cannot afford to start off on the wrong foot with your customers. The same has to be said of reports or any of the other persuasive writing projects you have in mind. Impact is crucial.

When you saw the heading 'Starting with impact', you may have thought that I simply meant a large splash of colour or a 'grab 'em' title, but impact can be far more subtle than that. Impact can be a blank screen, or a block of colour with no words, or it could be a scene. Impact can simply be whatever you want it to be – whatever suits your persuasive writing project.

Remember this

Invest effort into starting with impact. What do you want the reader to feel: shocked? curious? interested? Do you want to move them emotionally?

Two facts to get you thinking about your front cover or title:

> More books are sold with a title starting with 'The' than any other word.

> People love alliteration – Pride and Prejudice, Sense and Sensibility.

Titles matter!

Now to get back to starting with impact. Did you notice the sentence below it? It read:

This is the most important section in this chapter.

Was this the most important section? I don't know, but it kept you reading up to this point. It is a prime example of starting with impact, as most readers will have paid particular attention from there on – did you?

Keeping it simple

At this point in the book you may feel that it is all getting very complex and that there is a lot to take on board, but actually some of the most persuasive copy has been simple but teasing. Keeping it simple enables you to reach out to all your readers and some of the most stunning examples of simplicity have been the most effective. For example, plain black posters with the simple message 'It's coming...' had readers transfixed for weeks. What could it be? What was coming? It was actually a new mobile phone network. Similarly teasing hoardings may have only one word on such as 'What?' or 'Who?' Teasing the reader in this way intrigues them. It is incredibly effective and yet so simple.

Even simple enthusiasm can be very persuasive, as can a true story.

Remember this

You don't have to create complicated messages. Sometimes a simple message of one or two words – or even a single image with no words – can move people more than clever text (and remember that people need to engage emotionally with your message).

Being consistent

Check out your consistency. If you are presenting a message, it has to be consistent so that it does not confuse the reader. Consistency can be the style you use, the way you present your copy, your consistent message and so forth. Some companies will run campaigns in which a number of ads will follow a theme.

Remember this

Look through magazines or copy and start to recognize themes, fonts, logos, phrases and style that link a series of texts together. Every company wants something that is uniquely theirs because that is how they build a brand image. When you are proficient as a persuasive writer, you too may be asked to produce ideas and copy that creates a new brand image.

The notion of brand image is that it is instantly recognizable. There are certain logos, strap lines and styles that we all recognize from our favourite goods. They have been developed through time and very possibly started with a persuasive writer, like yourself, who came up with a great idea. However, it is essential that we are able to maintain that and be consistent. When brands move away from their unique method of communication, the readers are not always supportive and there can be complaints. Humans, in the main, like things to be consistent and that is why you should aim to build consistency into your writing style.

Grouping

Finally, in this section I would like you to think about grouping words and phrases together. Some wording groups just go together like patterns. For example, if I said to you 'Are you sitting comfortably?' the majority of people would expect 'Then I'll begin...' These are stock phrases and can be comforting for the reader as well as leading them on. I don't need to tell you that I am going to tell you a story, if I start my sentence 'Once upon a time...'

Another grouping of words that engages the reader is 'Do you want to hear a secret?' How many people would say no to that? These groupings of popular words can really help the persuasive writer to reach out to the reader and draw them in, without their realizing it.

Focus points

Writing is a highly effective method of communication whereby you can reach out and engage a whole range of readers and persuade them to focus on your message.

When writing persuasively we need to keep the reader firmly in our thoughts. Who are they? What would appeal to them? What type of words would they use?

There are a number of particular types of reader and categorizing them in this way can help the writer to focus more clearly and therefore change style to meet each need.

There is so much information around that we need to make our message stand out. We need to start off with impact to catch the reader's attention. This does not have to be an outrageous statement; it can be impact from colour or a lack of wording too.

Keep your message simple. You do not need convoluted or tricky wording; a simple message well thought through can be just as effective. Use this with other techniques such as grouping words and using familiar phrases and keep it consistent. You may be building a brand without realizing it!

Case studies

Let's see how Leonie and Paul are getting on.

Leonie is delighted to receive a letter inviting her to an interview and is even more surprised to find out that they will want her to do some activities on the day. Leonie has never done anything like this before. She looks at the job description again and notices that the job is in the marketing section of the organization and when she reads the letter more closely she realizes that they are putting her forward for a more senior role than the one for which she applied. Leonie is shocked but secretly excited; they think that she could do the job above the one she applied for! She must not disappoint them and so she decides to look into what is required for marketing. She writes back to accept the interview and starts to look for examples of marketing around the house. She picks up some magazines for inspiration. There seems to be so many styles. She flicks through and considers how the writer is reaching out to her, how the words and images engage, and she starts making notes about her ideas. She notices that some of the most arresting advertisements that catch her eye are the simplest – is there a lesson there?

Paul has worked hard to pull a report together with a spreadsheet of costings to show to Mr Pan at their next meeting. He feels confident in his data but feels that the whole project needs more 'sell' to interest his owner. The figures are certainly impressive and there is a lot of additional local business that could be theirs if they market themselves more effectively. However, apart from the figures, he is not sure how to get Mr Pan's attention. What if Mr Pan does not actually want to expand the business? After all, he does not seem to have tried to do so before. As he calls in at the house to collect his lunch from the refrigerator, he sees Mr Pan's daughter, Lizzie, drawing at the table and he has an idea. He asks her to draw him a poster advertising Pan Haulage to the local community. Lizzie is more than happy to do that, and Paul guesses that, by including his daughter in the process, he will at least hook Mr Pan sufficiently to explain the rest of his proposal. It is the 'hook' he had been looking for and so now all he needs is a way to start the project off with impact. He decides to do a split test with the other units on the site and sends some information labelled 'Haulage with Heart' to one side of the estate and 'From the family: for you' to the other side. He will see which one is the more effective and attracts the more attention.

Next step

In this chapter we have covered even more techniques that you can choose to consider. Some of them will be easy and fit into your work, others might be more suitable for other situations. Think through the ideas and weigh up which ones will be most beneficial to you. In the next chapter we will be looking at a specific subject: how you write to motivate others. This could be motivating them to do something, such as buy a product or take action in some way, or simply to make them feel good.

6

Writing to
Motivate

Goal – to be able to create a motivating feeling and a call to action.

Diagnostic test

Answer each question by choosing a number from 1 to 5. Nearer to 1 indicates that you feel this statement to be *false or incorrect* and nearer to 5 indicates that you feel it is *more likely to be true*.

I believe that people can motivate others

I believe that we all have the capacity for self-motivation

I understand that our motivation can vary in different aspects of our lives

Motivation is the magic formula that makes things happen

Some people need to be encouraged more than others

I believe that my writing can either get people excited or turn them off

Some words are naturally motivating

Some words suggest excitement and energy

I enjoy using words that pick people up

I believe that we can all write in a more motivating style if we want to

Now add up your score and see what it says about you.

Result

35–50   This score indicates that you are very aware of the impact your writing has on others. Perhaps you have already worked in advertising or marketing and are very aware that, by motivating the reader, you can make them take action. You are also aware that people like to be motivated and love to feel that they have made the right choice. Think about the pointers you have picked up so far and continue them into this chapter and – get motivating!

20–34   You may be a little unsure of what we mean by motivating someone with our writing and how that equates to their taking action. When using motivating copy we want the person to feel good about themselves. This can give them the energy to take action such as move a project along or take control of some part of their lives. Imagine that you have treated yourself to a small gift, or someone says 'Well done' for the work you have done; you feel happy, pleased and ready to face the day with a smile. That is what we mean by motivating copy.

Below 20   Your lower score here indicates that you are perhaps not sure that motivating copy will work for you. Maybe you have always worked on traditional documents and have not recognized the additional power that is hidden in words and the way they are grouped or placed on the page. Read through this chapter and research some areas where you may have been affected by motivating copy yourself. Now look back at your work, could you introduce some motivation into your work?

Have you ever read something and thought 'My goodness, I must do that right now' or even 'I must have that product now'? If so, you have been subject to motivational writing. Motivational writing is not just for sales copy and I hope to prove to you that you can introduce it into all areas of your life, even into your shopping list!

Remember this

Find something around you right now, something that you just had to have, whether that be an expensive item or the pot of salad for your lunch. Make a note of how you felt when you chose that item. For example, you may have thought you picked a pot of salad for lunch to quell your hunger, but why that particular pot? There must have been others there to choose from. How did you feel afterwards? Good about making the healthy choice? Good because you saved money because it was on offer?

Our feelings and thoughts drive our actions, and, when we feel good about ourselves, we start to feel good about life. When we feel that things are going well we achieve more, spend more, treat ourselves better and feel more healthy. Therefore people who are motivated are more upbeat, achieve more and simply get more things done.

What is motivation?

What got you out of bed this morning? What takes you into work or enables you to get a job done? It's motivation, but we don't always pay it the attention it deserves.

If we had no motivation we would not achieve anything of note; we might not even leave the covers of our comfy bed. People who are not motivated to do anything achieve very little. They also may lack energy because energy is linked to motivation; the two go together. Quite often, when we say we are motivated to do something we actually mean that we feel energized to do that thing. We suddenly have the energy to undertake specific tasks or to make changes to our lives. Without that energy we may be lacklustre and achieve very little. Therefore motivation is critically important in creating the energy to ensure progress.

Also, choice makes us feel good about ourselves. When we feel we have made the choice, and the outcome is good, then we also congratulate ourselves on our ability to make a good decision. It has been proven in psychological experiments that when we choose a product or course of action we are more likely to feel satisfied and that we have control over it, even if this strictly isn't true. We can see this in the example below:

▶ Example 1: 'Please complete the form below and send it to the following address'

▶ Example 2: 'Please complete the form below and either send to the following address or fax through to XXXX XXXXX'.

In the first example the reader does not have a choice and, although nothing will prevent a motivated person, a less motivated person may balk at being told what to do. In the second example the reader has a choice. They might still send the form by post but it is their decision to do so and therefore they automatically feel a greater sense of decision making. It is this sense of choice that creates more energy and fuels motivation.

(Notice that in this example the choice is to send the form this way or that way; there is not a choice to not send the form at all – that would be a choice we do not want to offer, because we are persuading them to send in the form. The choice in this example is therefore 'contained'.)

Key idea

Motivation and energy are linked. When, as persuasive writers, we want the reader to take action it can be helpful to offer them a choice so that they feel more in control.

Why creating motivation is important

The art of persuasive writing suggests that we, the writer, need to persuade the reader to do something. This could be anything from asking for a sale through to requesting a form, as in the example above. Why do we need to do that? Surely, if the product is good enough to engage the reader, they will want to buy the product, or carry out the action we request? Well, actually we are back to signposting the reader to let them know what you would like them to do next, not because we are asking anything unreasonable or extreme, but because the reader is busy and this is just another thing that we are asking them to do. Do you remember earlier on in this book that I said that so much information is competing for our attention? With the best will in the world, many readers will be distracted by other pressures and may forget to return to the action that both of you intended them to take.

We need to keep our readers on track and with their full attention until we direct them otherwise.

Remember this

Think about the last time you read some sales copy and thought 'I must order that' or 'I must try that' – only to forget ten minutes later. How did that feel at the time? Do you feel guilty about it now?

It is no good to us as writers of copy if readers intend to take action but then don't. We want solid action and sometimes the reader needs a bit of helpful coaxing, reminding and help.

This can be provided in many forms. To start off, ask yourself these questions:

- ▶ Am I being clear about the action I want my reader to take?

- ▶ Is the reader clear about the action I want them to take?

- ▶ Have I made it very simple for my reader to take that action?

- ▶ Have I given them choice (if applicable)?

- ▶ Have I repeated this message or delivered it in several different ways?

- ▶ Have I finished off by repeating the 'next step' once again?

These questions will not cover every situation but they will be helpful for most.

Why are we asking people to take action? Well, the fact that the reader is engaged in your prose and is paying attention to your writing demonstrates that they are interested in what you have to say (at some level). So many people never achieve their potential in life because achieving what you want can seem scary and it is easier to back off. Also, not everyone is completely sure how to go about organizing how to get what they want. This is another reason why creating motivation is so very important. They need you to stand beside them and metaphorically hold their hand or provide some encouragement. The truth is that they may not take that next step without you by their side and therefore we need to build motivation into our writing.

Remember this

Not everyone is sufficiently self-motivated to snap up your ideas. Change can be quite scary for many people. They may need help and this can be provided by including motivational triggers within your writing.

Nothing happens without motivation and therefore we need to encourage our readers to make that move!

Motivating words

Motivation is about energy and so let's look at some words that scream ENERGY at the reader:

Wow!	Sexy	Electrifying
Dynamic	Riveting	Pulse-racing
Exciting	Trail-blazing	Stimulating
Awesome	Explosive	Jaw-dropping
Compelling	Earth-shattering	Sizzling
Invigorating	Raw power	Turbo-charged
Mesmerizing	Fantastic	Dynamite
Powerful	Hypnotic	Thrilling

However, when writing persuasively, being able to create energy and enthusiasm is only half the story. We also need to remove any obstacles that might creep in the way in an attempt to minimize the risk of a blockage coming between the reader and our message. We are talking here about answering the 'Ah buts' that litter the reader's thinking, while they are still reading. These invasive critters can come in and destroy all our good work if we are not careful. Therefore we need to quell these voices by offering assurance to the reader, by using words such as:

Tried	Tested	Guarantee
Authentic	Innovative	Promise
Investment	Rare	Endorsed
Stylish	Satisfying	Original
Certified	Credible	Safe

These words (and others like them) both lower the level of perceived risk and also offer consolation to those wary of making a commitment. If your persuasive writing includes a few of each subset of words, it will be taking the 'dual' approach. Individually these words are powerful and motivating, but linked together they hold a greater force. For example:

> **Complete the form NOW and you will be one of the elite taking the first step towards achieving your new future. Every entry is underwritten by our famous GUARANTEE so that you simply cannot lose. Think how awesome it will be when you start to...**

and so forth.

Let's look at how that paragraph is constructed:

> **Complete the form *NOW* {energy} and you will be *one of the elite taking the first step* {motivation} towards *achieving your new future* {motivation}. Every entry is underwritten by our famous *GUARANTEE* {obstacle removing} so that you simply *cannot lose* {obstacle removing}. Think how *awesome* {energy} it will be when you start to...**

I'm sure you could work on this again to improve it even further, but for now it is a recipe with some good ingredients.

To take this up to the next level, consider words that simply sound lovely, such as 'silk', 'cashmere', 'sublime' or 'sensual'. When we read we hear the words in our heads. If you watch small children you will notice that they actually read the words out to themselves. As they get older they move towards just their lips moving and finally to be able to read 'in their head' but, even when we no longer move our lips with the sound, we still retain the notion of hearing the words in our heads. That is why words that sound wonderful can also be considered motivating. I recently asked a friend to take part in a blind product test for me. I gave her four soaps to try out and, to cover up their real names, I renamed them. The one she chose as her favourite I had named 'soft and creamy' and she had to admit that the name was partly the reason for selecting that soap as a winner. She said it just sounded so luxurious; such is the power of words!

Remember this

What other words can you think of that would create energy in your reader? Which ones jump out to you? Which ones would personally motivate you into taking some action?

Motivating phrases

Groups of words can be even more motivating than one word. Consider the phrase:

> **You know you want it...**

It positively reeks of temptation and brings to mind Oscar Wilde's famous line, 'I can resist everything except temptation' – and most of your readers will feel the same.

What about:

Don't you deserve the best?

Who is going to think 'No' to that? Even if we don't give an outright 'Yes' we will be significantly intrigued to read further or start questioning – and that is all the motivation you need.

Or how about:

Join the smart group of investors who have chosen to join this scheme...

Don't you want to be considered smart? One of this elite group? The implication here is that if you are part of this set of people you will be considered to be smart and savvy – and all you have to do is complete a form to join their scheme. What could be simpler?

Extending it further, who could resist:

Go on, do it! You know you want to...

Or even:

Resistance is futile, so go on, do it now...

Do you recognize any of these phrases? You may have seen similar ones advertising goods or services, and the reason they are used over and over again is that they work. Obviously they would not be suitable for a business report, but they may well be used effectively in advertising.

Key idea

Creating motivational phrases can help drive more people to take action or to respond to your suggestions. Writing motivational phrases with a cheeky twist can even cause them to laugh as they do so, but the important aspect is encouraging action.

The importance of appearance

The appearance of your words is hugely important – I mean HUGELY IMPORTANT!!!!

Can you see the difference? I certainly don't mean that your messages should scream out at the reader, but there is a case for using a few tricks to convey attitude, meaning and inference. So let's look at some ideas that you can use straight away:

Capital letters – they always look like they are shouting at you and so use them very carefully to accentuate certain points. For example, look at the following paragraphs and see which one you think would bring the best rewards:

Example 1

> GREAT OFFER
>
> For one day only we can offer you something special. We can offer you two items for the price of one. This offer is so generous that we usually only offer it to our key customers once a year, but we have had so much good fortune lately, we have decided to pass it on to all our customers, and that includes you.

Example 2

> GREAT OFFER
>
> FOR ONE DAY ONLY WE CAN OFFER YOU SOMETHING SPECIAL. WE CAN OFFER YOU TWO ITEMS FOR THE PRICE OF ONE. THIS OFFER IS SO GENEROUS THAT WE USUALLY ONLY OFFER IT TO OUR KEY CUSTOMERS ONCE A YEAR, BUT WE HAVE HAD SO MUCH GOOD FORTUNE LATELY, WE HAVE DECIDED TO PASS IT ON TO ALL OUR CUSTOMERS, AND THAT INCLUDES YOU.

Example 3

> **GREET OFFER**
>
> For ONE DAY ONLY we can offer you SOMETHING SPECIAL. We can offer you TWO ITEMS for the PRICE OF ONE. This offer is SO GENEROUS that we usually only offer it to our key customers once a year, but we have had so much good fortune lately, we have decided to pass it on to all our customers, and that includes YOU.

Let's see if we agree. I think that Example 1 is fine but nothing jumps out at me or draws my attention. Example 2 gives me a headache – all that shouting, and it is very difficult to read. Of these examples I would choose Example 3 as being the best copy because the use of both upper and lower case makes some words jump out at me. I simply cannot ignore them and of course they are the words that the persuasive writer wants me to notice.

Can we make those words stand out even more? Sure, we can embolden them:

> **GREET OFFER**
>
> For **ONE DAY ONLY** we can offer you **SOMETHING SPECIAL**. We can offer you **TWO ITEMS** for the **PRICE OF ONE**. This offer is **SO GENEROUS** that we usually only offer it to our key customers once a year, but we have had so much good fortune lately, we have decided to pass it on to all our customers, and that includes **YOU**.

Now let's look at that heading, the spacing and the sizing.

GREAT OFFER

For **ONE DAY ONLY** we can offer you **SOMETHING SPECIAL**. We can offer you **TWO ITEMS** for the **PRICE OF ONE**. This offer is **SO GENEROUS** that we usually only offer it to our key customers once a year, but we have had so much good fortune lately, we have decided to pass it on to all our customers, and that includes **YOU**.

In this example I have centred the text. I also increased the size of the emboldened words (just in case the reader missed them), by just one point size and increased the heading and final word by slightly more.

I will now just add the finishing touches – some punctuation and flourishes. I don't always like centred text but in this case I wanted the final word to end up in the middle, on its own line. I also wanted the emboldened words to sit together, not as in the previous example, when 'so' was on one line and 'generous' fell onto the following line.

*** GREAT OFFER ***

For **ONE DAY ONLY** we can offer you **SOMETHING SPECIAL**. We can offer you **TWO ITEMS** for the **PRICE OF ONE**. This offer is **SO GENEROUS** that we usually only offer it to our key customers once a year, but we have had so much good fortune lately, we have decided to pass it on to all our customers, and that includes...

YOU!

We could work on this further by tightening the message so that it is more succinct; for example:

*** GREAT OFFER ***

For **ONE DAY ONLY** we can offer you **SOMETHING SPECIAL**. We can offer you **TWO ITEMS** for the **PRICE OF ONE**. This offer is **SO GENEROUS** that we usually only offer it to our key customers once a year, and this year that includes...

YOU!

Now we are getting somewhere!

Remember this

You can continue perfecting, trimming, spacing and enhancing until you feel that you have reached the point when your copy is ready. There are no hard and fast rules to this – you stop when you feel it conveys the message you want to give.

Introducing motivational writing into your work

I have given you some examples in this chapter but you may have felt that they do not pertain to business use. I therefore intend this section to be exclusively for introducing motivational language into business use.

Remember this

Even though we will touch on this subject here, all of Chapter 10 focusses on using persuasive techniques in the workplace, including motivation, with many examples.

When you are using motivational techniques at work it is important to focus not just on attracting attention, but also on what you want the reader to be motivated to do. You then need to use the same techniques that are covered in this chapter, but soften them for the business environment. For example you would exchange:

Do it now!

for:

I would like to invite you to...

You could also include intriguing questions such as:

Have you ever considered how much you would save?

This piques the interest sufficiently to encourage the reader to read more. Or with flattery:

As a top manager your eye will always be on the budget, so let me show you how much you can save...

Who would say 'I'm not a top manager'? They are more likely to think 'Yes, that's me' and read on in the belief that the writer is talking directly to them.

Finally, remember that focus:

The benefits to us of using this product are XYZ – but only if we move swiftly on it. Therefore I suggest we immediately...

Notice in this example how the writer lulls the reader by spelling out the benefits and then moves swiftly onto the action they require, giving it a sense of urgency.

Key idea

Suggest the motivation you want to happen couched in softer tones so that it is more acceptable to your audience.

Focus points

Motivation is important in creating energy in our readers.

Readers with energy will take action and that means responding to your message.

Certain words are highly motivating, but we also need reassuring words to ensure that we wipe out any fears the reader might have before they take hold and prevent them taking action.

Keep revisiting your work by looking at presentation techniques to draw attention to your whole message and also key aspects of it. You can continue to refine and define until you feel that your work is ready for the reader. If you are worried, test out two versions, as mentioned in the previous chapter.

Recognize that motivational writing can enter any work situation; it does not have to be just for advertising.

Case studies

Let's see how Leonie and Paul are getting on.

When Leonie reaches Sullivans, she is impressed by their offices. She really feels excited by this opportunity and decides then and there that she *must* work here, in whatever capacity. While she is waiting in the foyer to meet someone from personnel, she watches the other staff. They all look so polished and successful and seem to know exactly what they are doing. Leonie does not find this disconcerting; on the contrary she finds it reassuring and it makes her feel safe. When she is invited in to meet the Personnel Officer she shakes her warmly by the hand and settles down for what she hopes will be a positive conversation. The Personnel Officer asks Leonie why she wants to work there and Leonie tells her how she wants to work with a stimulating team to create copy and advertisements that win people over. The Personnel Officer asks Leonie what she feels are the important components of 'winning people over' and, inspired by her recent thoughts while preparing for this interview, Leonie tells her that she feels that the copy must tap into people's emotions to motivate them to take some form of action. 'After all,' she adds, 'since coming here, I am motivated to want to provide the best interview I can, so that I can work here.' This time, for Leonie, the interview seems to be going well.

The split test told Paul that 'Haulage with Heart' was the heading to go for and so now he has his hook and headline. However, he has not approached Mr Pan just yet. He recognizes that to be successful there has to be some action. Mr Pan is a great talker and the danger is that he will be engaged, listen and be amused by the project, but then he might decide to wait, or need time to think about it, at which point the idea goes somewhat 'off the boil'. Paul knows that he needs to motivate Mr Pan to take action, or at the very least delegate that action to him. Whichever way, he needs Mr Pan to feel compelled to make a decision. He happens to hear of a 'take your daughter to work day' that is coming up in one month's time. He wonders if the local newspaper would run a story on 'Haulage with Heart,' link the story of Lizzie and announce their offer to other local family businesses. The paper said it would be very interested. Suddenly Paul has even more reason for Mr Pan to say yes. The project will be fully advertised, Lizzie will be in the newspaper and the newspaper will provide free advertising and coverage. Better still, Mr Pan cannot delay his decision because 'take your daughter to work day' is coming up fast and, with the newspaper needing to know its main stories in plenty of time, Mr Pan will have to make a decision quickly. Surely Mr Pan will not back down or procrastinate, will he?

 Next step

In this chapter we have specifically studied motivators that stimulate some form of action. Some of these may be the exchange of simple, passive words into their more exciting equivalent to create energy and drive and we have also looked at groups of words that increase the chance that the reader will take action. Finally, we have seen how Leonie and Paul are considering motivation in their own situations and realizing its importance. In the next chapter we will be exploring how to form a cohesive argument to further win people over.

Presenting a Cohesive Argument

Goal – to be able to present writing that persuades through following a reasoned argument.

Diagnostic test

Answer each question by choosing a number from 1 to 5. Nearer to 1 indicates that you feel this statement to be *false or incorrect* and nearer to 5 indicates that you feel it is *more likely to be true*.

I feel confident that I can structure a written argument

I believe that presenting a well defined argument is important for success

Written arguments can better help the reader to understand the points raised

Written arguments are an attempt to persuade

Written arguments present various points of view

I feel comfortable presenting points of view other than my own

I feel I need to answer my reader's questions

Presenting a cohesive argument is just another way of persuading the reader

I prefer longer text to explain my points

I like to have the opportunity to tell the whole story

Now add up your score and see what it says about you.

Result

35–50   This score indicates that, not only are you happy to present your argument in full to the reader, in fact you relish doing so. You believe that a well-structured and cohesive argument is not aggressive and can win people over to your point of view. For you, this offers the perfect opportunity to represent your ideas, product or service – and be able to justify, in full, what you are presenting. If this rings true for you, then read this chapter quickly as there may be one or two items in here that you may not have thought through.

20–34   This score indicates that you may be a little unsure of what we mean by producing a cohesive argument.

Perhaps you thought that arguing is aggressive or something that we, as persuasive writers, should avoid. After all, there is nothing very persuasive in getting all het up! Read through the chapter and you will see this is not what we mean at all. To clarify, every aspect of this chapter is geared towards persuading the reader; therefore, consider the points raised and see where you can integrate them into your work.

Below 20   Your lower score here indicates that you are perhaps not sure that persuading someone with an argument is the right way to go about things. Perhaps you consider arguments to be aggressive, but that is not what we mean here at all. What we want to do is to present the case for the product or service and hopefully help the reader to see why they should think that this is a good idea. Read through this chapter and then take the Diagnostic test once again. I am sure you will see a difference.

After the previous chapter, you may have thought that the only way to motivate the reader into action is to trim your words down in number and then replace some less exciting words with others that have more energy. Well, that is one way, but not the only way. That method works well for those who like small advertisements and sound bites, but in some circumstances a longer piece is required to fully persuade the reader to take action.

Remember this

Pick up a magazine or newspaper. The headlines will catch your eye, but notice that some adverts are quite small and many publications now have longer features that take the reader through an entertaining and sometimes informative read, while simultaneously delivering their message. In your work, what would you use the smaller, snappier writing for and when would you choose longer copy?

In this chapter we will consider when longer copy is more suitable and how to structure copy of this nature so that it leads the reader through to a satisfying conclusion. Hopefully the reader will also have learned something along the way and you, the writer, have had the opportunity to relay your message effectively and possibly stimulate some action on the part of the reader.

What is a cohesive argument?

Cohesive – co-he-sive

Connected or related in a reasonable way to form a whole

Uniting people or things

Argument – ar-gu-ment

[countable] a set of reasons that show that something is true or untrue

(Source: *Longman Dictionary of Contemporary English*)

Therefore a cohesive argument is a feature that enables the writer to convey a number of aspects relating to their message, in a connected way that ultimately proves (or disproves) the point they wish to make.

It is also important to note that the term 'argument' used here does not describe a disagreement or conflict. It is a conversation that the writer simply cannot have with every reader. In reality it is the writer arguing their particular point through the medium of words – and in turn convincing the reader that the writer's stance is the correct one. In other words, it is a piece of persuasive copy.

Do not think for one moment that this type of copy is simply dashed off; these features are carefully crafted to lead the reader on a specific journey that will enable them to reach the destination specified by the writer. They can be bright and breezy or thought provoking, or even lull the reader into a hypnotic trance of comfort and ease. What they all have in common is that the writers are, at all times, aware of the effect the writing has on the reader and where they are leading the reader on a journey of progression.

Key idea

Not all persuasive writing is short messages. Sometimes longer copy is required to convey complex ideas, or to build the reader up to a crescendo of desperation to act on your suggestions immediately. Consider the most appropriate way to transmit your messages; shorter is not always better.

Why and when should we be using one?

There are generally three reasons for using this approach in our persuasive writing:

On occasions our message may be quite complex and we may need to explain certain issues and approaches. This can result in our maybe having to go back in time to explain how a situation has come to this point. You are therefore relaying history before moving on to the issue in hand and that takes time.

We may need to take time to engage with the reader, and, to help this, we may need to explain about ourselves, our own background and our credibility before we even move on to explain about our message.

We may need to draw the reader in s-l-o-w-l-y for certain topics and this requires us to lay the foundations in full, building on them, one element at a time.

We should not be using the cohesive argument approach when we want fast impact, as it takes time to read through a cohesive argument and come to a view. Therefore it is best suited to either complex or longer pieces where explanation is necessary.

Remember this

Look at the cohesive approach taken below. Notice how it is longer than my previous examples and takes time to persuade the reader that they need to attend. It explains every step of the programme (shortened to just the first few words in my example) and finishes with a call to action – with pressure.

Have you ever felt that you really don't want to work, that you would rather spend your time more meaningfully? Then you are just like me and thousands of others that I meet every day.

Have you ever thought, if only I could find more time to develop interests of my own? That alone would give you more time to spend with friends or that special hobby that has become neglected.

Well, magic wands are in short supply but I would like to share a secret with you that has made my life ten times richer and it really is very simple. So simple in fact that you can do it yourself and create the life that you want.

Imagine all that additional time… what would you do? A neglected hobby? More time with family? Or how about more time in the garden or lazing with a book?

At this stage I realize that you must be thinking that 'this is too good to be true' – but it really isn't. In the past year I have helped hundreds of people discover the door to their perfect lives. This really must be one of life's biggest secrets and I am willing to share it with you!

Are you thinking 'this is just a sales letter'? Then let Mrs Jones from Lancaster tell you 'I turned my life around with this technique' and Michael Forster from Manchester adds 'This was one decision I am so glad I took.'

I still feel you are not convinced and so I will tell you what we will be covering on this programme:

▶ First we will…

▶ Following that we will…

▶ I will take you personally by the hand and walk you through…

▶ Together we will rid you of….

▶ I'm going to help YOU uncover…

Still feeling unconvinced? Don't worry, here is a link so that you can read other people's experiences of the day. {www.linkandallthat}

Worried about being dissatisfied? I don't blame you but this programme is all backed by my full MONEY BACK GUARANTEE. How can you lose? It's simply impossible! Even from the moment of booking, you will feel that your life is on track once again.

This offer may not come your way again, and backed by our full MONEY BACK GUARANTEE it is a no brainer! Email your acceptance NOW!

Make the decision to change your life today, because this offer may end tomorrow.

Notice how I have tried to anticipate any of the arguments that may be offered up by the reader and quelled them by explanation (what is covered on the programme) and by facing the reader straight on ('You may be wondering…'). This way the reader would really have to struggle hard to find reasons for not taking me up on this fantastic offer.

Remember this

These cohesive arguments are deliberately written to win you over and they do it gently through reason and explanation.

The advertorial

Advertorials have been entering our magazines and journals for some time now. In fact you may have read hundreds of them and not even realized what they are. Advertorials are so called because they are somewhere between an advert and an editorial. The first thing you immediately notice about them is that they look just like an editorial feature. They may even have a celebrity on the page and look like an interview – but make no mistake, they are written as sales copy.

Advertorials are not objective; they are written by persuasive writers and they aim to advertise a product or service in a longer, cohesively argued manner. All journalists keep to the advice given through Kipling's 'Six Honest Serving Men', namely that copy should include:

- ▶ **What** – what is the article about? What should we be concerned or interested about? What should I do next?

- ▶ **Why** – why are you reading this? Why we should be interested or concerned? Why did something happen?

- ▶ **When** – when did the fact happen? When should I be concerned about this?

- ▶ **How** – how did these things come about? How should they be addressed? How can I change things?

- ▶ **Where** – where is all this happening? Where can I get the answer to my problems?

- ▶ **Who** – who can I contact?

Key idea

Kipling's 'Six Honest Serving Men' is a poem to enable anyone to check that their copy includes all the relevant facts. If you were to pick up any major newspaper and look at the lead story it would include all these six on the front page.

This formula for content is exactly the same with advertorials. They need to contain all of these aspects if they are to be a complete article. These 'Six Honest Serving Men' also provide a framework (or aide-memoire) for ensuring that both your editorial and your advertorial contain all that is needed for the reader to feel fulfilled and enable them to take action.

The aim of the advertorial is to seduce the reader to take action through the relationship they have with the magazine. All magazines are aimed at specifically identified groups, based on certain factors such as age, salary, newspaper readership and location. From this information the marketing professional will construct a profile of the 'typical reader'. This then enables the magazine to target their advertisements at a certain readership for greater results (marketing staff will not put advertisements into magazines that do not have the correct readership profile for their product or service). For example, you would not advertise mother and baby products in a man's lifestyle magazine, or stair lifts in a magazine aimed at the young woman of today. OK, so the occasional reader may be interested, but advertising is about attracting volume; if you cannot guarantee that a lot of readers will be interested, then it is usually no dice.

Most readers identify with their magazine choice and feel that the magazine says something about them. They are therefore happy to carry the magazine and be seen reading it. The advertorial taps into this relationship by sidling up to them like a best friend while feeding views and information on products that may sound impartial – but are not.

Remember this

Advertorials have to state somewhere on the page that they are an advert or an advertorial so that the reader is in no doubt that the writer is not writing a neutral feature, but one that is heavily biased towards promoting a product – however, these statements can be small and difficult to find on the page.

Structure is king

With any cohesive argument we are looking to persuade the reader and bring them around to our point of view. In fact we may even start by agreeing with them, which will provide that all-important hook, before arguing for the opposite; but, just as in any formal discussion, the writing must have structure.

The structure of the example given earlier in this chapter is to start with an attempt to hook the reader (in this instance by offering statements that the reader would agree with). Paragraph three shows a jokey, friendly comment about magic wands (who has never wanted one of those?). Paragraph four introduces some fairly regular time fantasies that people have (note that they are deliberately general as I want the argument to appeal to as many people as possible). Paragraph five acknowledges that we may have drifted away from reality (together) and that it is time to add a teaser – remember at this point the reader does not know what the product is. Notice the attempt to get close to the reader with the offer to share a secret – we all love secrets. Paragraph six introduces two endorsements, which may or may not be real; the reader cannot know whether they are at this stage, but you, the writer, are their friend and so it is likely that they will accept them. It is only when we arrive at the bulleted list that the detail is outlined. It is then followed up by a call to action, with the added pressure of a time limit.

We could easily turn that feature into an advertorial by, perhaps, adding a celebrity endorsement. Imagine the same feature but now with a photo (no additional quotes) of your favourite celebrity in the top corner; does it now start to feel as if they are speaking directly to you? Do you feel tempted? Would your favourite celebrity hold these secrets? Is that how they became famous? Goodness, we are now reading all manner of information into that simple copy, but you can see that it follows a structure.

Key idea

If you were to persuade a friend to start coming to the gym with you twice a week, how would you do it? Would you leap in with the suggestion? Probably not. You would think about what you thought their objections would be and think through some suitable answers. You would then approach the subject gently, possibly even by flattering them, or planting the seed of an idea first.

Arguments, in a written form, are well-structured attempts to build a relationship with the reader so that they accept the information, while simultaneously giving your opinion in the most acceptable form. The desired outcome is to persuade the reader that you are their friend, ask them to trust you with data and then test them, by asking for an action.

Don't forget to play with the words

Try it now

Look back over the argument featured earlier. Do you agree with my choice of words? You might have chosen different ones.

When I wrote the cohesive argument shown earlier I deliberately stayed clear of capital letters and over-exciting, dramatic words because I wanted to be genuine and win the reader's confidence. You may decide that, had you written it, you would have used different words – that is your prerogative as a writer. (If it were a celebrity advertorial, it would help to use the type of language that the celebrity endorsing it would use. For example, if writing for a pension product featuring an older TV celebrity I would not use phrases such as BUY IT NOW!!! – unless the person actually spoke like that.)

Words are your tool. Make them appropriate to:

▶ the readership

▶ the situation

▶ any character endorsement.

If you are not happy with the result, rewrite again and again until you feel it produces a convincing and cohesive argument.

You're leading me on!

Well, yes I am. Writing advertorials or cohesive arguments is a skill that you can easily learn and it could reap you great benefits. Whether you tone it down for a business document or tighten it up for an advertisement, you will be taking your reader by the hand and leading them through your argument. When they fall into step beside you, then you know that they will follow you anywhere.

Remember this

Not everyone has the time or inclination to read advertorials or cohesive argument copy, but, when someone does, it is easier for them to become involved because you commence a relationship with the reader. By the end they want to follow you and some will even see you as their friend. You therefore have a responsibility to be honest and professional in all your copy.

I have mentioned throughout this book that persuasive writing techniques must be used with care and responsibility. Leading your readers is very different from misleading your readers and you need to make sure that you act ethically at all times. Any hint that you may be exploiting your readers or taking advantage of them will actually lose you readers and this you cannot afford to do.

Focus points

Producing a cohesive argument is a skill that can be used by anyone, in any situation.

Overcoming objections is a key part of producing a cohesive argument; therefore you need to be able to anticipate those objections in advance of presenting your argument.

Producing an advertorial is one way of creating a cohesive argument that looks like an editorial. It is based on the relationship that the reader has with the magazine and/or celebrity (if an endorsement is used). Any celebrity link must be appropriate.

Consider how you would structure an argument if you knew you wanted to gain someone's agreement to something. You would not jump in; you would approach the subject in your own way and might even flatter them or suggest some other ideas first. These are the strategies you need to consider using with your readers.

Once you have your structure in outline and your initial text in place, edit by reconsidering every word to make sure your tone is exactly right.

Case studies

Let's see how Leonie and Paul use cohesive arguments in their workplace.

Leonie is surprised when the personnel officer tells her that, as part of her interview, she must undertake a piece of work. Leonie is worried because she has never worked in advertising or marketing before and her CV makes this clear. Will they expect her to know tricks or special techniques? How can she possibly be a success in this?

Leonie is taken to a room and asked to write a convincing argument why the company should employ her. At first she is stumped; what can she say? It seems arrogant to write about yourself like this. Suddenly she has an idea. Leonie has read many magazines and decides to write an advertorial in the form of an interview, with herself as the subject. Writing it this way, the words flow and she realizes that she automatically has a structure provided by the questions. When she hands it back she feels confident that she has done a good job (even if she is not sure that this is exactly what they wanted). The personnel officer looks at it briefly and Leonie thinks that she detects a smile in her eyes, but is not sure; after all, she has never done anything quite like this before.

Paul decides to hold a meeting with Mr Pan to outline his proposals. He returns to his original focus: he wants to persuade Mr Pan to allow him to build the business, starting locally. He is aware that Mr Pan does not like change and also that the business makes a reasonable turnover already. Mr Pan likes safety and quite rightly would not jeopardize his current market share on a whim. This new proposal must show Mr Pan how this could enhance his business, will be low risk and will not endanger his current customer base. Paul has also noted that Mr Pan needs to consider requests in his own time; he likes to 'sleep on the matter' and so Paul plans his approach. He writes a business plan for Pan's Haulage and includes all his ideas around 'Haulage with Heart' – he even writes a fictitious feature for the newspaper as an advertorial featuring Lizzie so that Mr Pan can get a full picture of how the programme could be launched. He goes back over his report and decides to choose safe words rather than their more exciting equivalents, so that it suits Mr Pan's style. He also up-plays the 'family' aspect and reduces any 'money making' aspect. For example, rather than state that the business wishes to expand, he majors on it reaching out to the community. As well as the report, Paul has booked a meeting with Mr Pan so that he can deliver his idea in person, the report being the document that Mr Pan takes away for future reading. Paul is really excited. He believes that he has one shot at this and so he practises his presentation and how he can present a cohesive argument.

Next step

In this chapter we have looked not only at how to construct a cohesive argument (including Kipling's 'Six Honest Serving Men') but also at when and where to use this approach. Cohesive arguments can be forceful or can take a much more relaxed approach to your persuasive writing, but they still require careful consideration at every stage. In the next chapter we will be considering the production of sales copy and how getting a grip on this very up-front way of presenting words can help boost your business.

8

Producing
Sales Copy

Goal – to identify and incorporate techniques that lead to sales.

Diagnostic test

Answer each question by choosing a number from 1 to 5. Nearer to 1 indicates that you feel this statement to be *false or incorrect* and nearer to 5 indicates that you feel it is *more likely to be true*.

I feel happy with producing sales copy

I believe that people want to buy goods and services

I buy goods and services based on advertisements and advertorials

I feel confident producing copy that sells

I understand the tools and techniques that I can use

I feel comfortable selling as long as I know that I am offering credible goods and services

I recognize that some advertisements are more successful than others

Writing sales copy can be great fun

I believe that sales copy is a useful marketing tool

I like to think that I have contributed towards company success and customer satisfaction

Now add up your score and see what it says about you.

Result

35–50   This score indicates that not only are you aware of the link between sales and company success, but you also enjoy the creative process. Writing good sales copy is a skill that is welcome anywhere. A company might offer the best products in the world but, if they are not marketed efficiently or sold, then there is no future for that company. Therefore, writers who can persuade customers to buy goods and services are highly prized. Read through this chapter to see if there are more ways of increasing your knowledge in this fascinating area of persuasive writing.

20–34   This score indicates that you may not be quite so comfortable with writing sales copy. Perhaps you like the idea of persuasive writing but not straight sales copy, or maybe you don't like to feel that you are pressurizing people. If either of these is you, then this chapter will do two things for you. It will show you that writing sales copy is a skill and you will learn the tools and techniques of that skill. It will also show you that in no way are you pressurizing the customer. If they wish they can simply put the copy down and walk away from it.

Below 20   Your lower score here indicates that you are either not happy or lacking confidence in writing sales copy. Perhaps you fear that the goods you are selling are not of sufficient quality, or you worry that there will be a backlash from customers. There is much that can be done to alleviate those fears and therefore you should read through the following chapter and undertake all of the exercises. Most writers are asked to write some form of sales copy at some point in their lives and it would be helpful to know some of the skills and techniques.

In writing a book about persuasive writing it would be impossible not to include sales techniques. Not all persuasive writing is sales based and you may be persuading someone to take some other action, but a proportion of your persuasive copy will definitely be sales related.

Remember this

Think back to the last object or service that you bought. Did you buy it independently or were you sold it through advertising or persuasive copy? Think hard – was it a truly independent purchase or were you 'nudged' into action?

We all read and react to sales data. It is the only way we know about any new development, product or service. As we have already seen through advertorials, even magazine features that appear as information can carry sales copy embedded within their folds. Sales writing is neither good nor bad – and neither is the writer. We all have times in our lives when we need to sell, whether that be ourselves in a CV for a job, our old car or the children's toys when they grow up and so being able to construct sales copy is a useful life skill too. The most effective sales copy will draw the maximum number of responses and therefore it is worth putting some effort into polishing the finished item.

It is also important to note that the techniques covered in this chapter are not just for selling products and service. You can also use them to sell your ideas to your manager or colleagues.

Remember this

Think about the last time you had to 'sell' an idea to someone. Did you really think about how you were going to structure your pitch? Did you consider the 'what's in it for them' question and then work this into your approach?

Let's take a look at what you need to remember.

Following AIDA

AIDA is a well-known copywriting mnemonic that describes a formula. AIDA stand for:

▶ A – attract **ATTENTION**

▶ I – arouse **INTEREST**

▶ D – stimulate the **DESIRE** to purchase

▶ A – prompt the reader to take **ACTION**.

Let's look at these four areas in more detail:

Attention – I have mentioned earlier that there are many distractions in everyone's life. When you are next on a train journey, look at all the posters both inside the train and in the station, all vying for our attention. To stand a chance of anyone buying from you, you have to get their attention. This can be in the form of a headline, a visual image (such as a picture or colour combination) or even a sound. Certain themes also attract our attention. For example, if I were to state 'I had a row with another author while at a conference', that would get your attention. Conflict is something that (rightly or wrongly) we appear to be highly attuned to – that is why you will see so many magazines with an attention-grabbing headline such as 'Author Bust Up!'

Interest – having gained the reader's attention, the next step is to arouse interest. Even effective attention-grabbing techniques will not maintain interest if there is not something for the reader. People buy products or services because they believe that they will gain something from them. There are certain subjects that are perennially popular:

▶ losing weight

▶ increasing your income

▶ saving money

▶ living longer

▶ being more attractive

▶ better relationships

▶ improving your life or your career prospects

▶ being able to out-perform others.

This is not a definitive list, but, if you are able to link your sales copy or advertisement to any of these factors, the likelihood of maintaining interest is increased.

Desire – having aroused the person's interest you now need to stimulate their desire to buy your product or service. Your aim here is to make the offer so irresistible that the reader becomes excited and cannot wait to place their order. This is the point when you introduce offers and demonstrate testimonials or quotes from experts. By showing that the product or service really does meet their needs, you will stimulate the desire for action on behalf of the buyer – but beware, they have not placed that order, or picked up the phone just yet.

Action – you must be clear and tell the buyer what you want them to do to take action – and make that next step as easy as possible for them. For example:

> **Don't delay, ring XXX XXXXX or send a text to XXX NOW for your immediate quote.**

Creating a multiple sales strategy

Your sales copy should form part of a sales plan. That is a structured and co-ordinated programme of introducing your ideas. Well-written sales copy will generate sales, but, if it is combined with other sales promotions, it will not only create greater sales but also start to create a brand in the customer's mind.

Let's go back to our pizza shop example. I talked earlier in this book about creating an eye-catching leaflet that could be posted through doors with the intention of it being retained by the home owner for future reference. Imagine now that we decide to follow that up with a poster campaign so that the home owners will see the name and product again, perhaps on their way home from work. They will be hungry and the poster will remind them that the leaflet to order pizza is in the kitchen drawer.

Remember this

Think for a moment. What other ideas could you add to your multiple sales strategy? They have to be ideas that promote the message and prompt action.

In the exercise above you could have detailed any number of ideas, but some that you may have had could include:

- website advertising
- text messaging
- free gifts such as pens or fridge magnets
- discount vouchers (perhaps offered through complementary stores such as media rental shops)
- logo beer mats in pubs

to name but a few.

While we are considering this multiple sales strategy it is worth mentioning that you can overdo it, so choose your strategy carefully. Also, never antagonize the customer. Sending unsolicited emails is spamming and if you continue to send emails without permission you will get in trouble. Another example of annoying customers is sending advertising faxes. These cost the customer money in fax paper. Thankfully, as fewer organizations still use faxes, this practice is going out of fashion.

Key idea

All multiple sales strategies have to have consistent themes and complement each other.

What we mean by this is that, when your multiple sales strategy is designed so that each activity complements each other in look, type and feel, that is when you start to create a brand.

For example, imagine that you were organizing a wedding. You might decide to have a theme of butterflies. With that in mind you would want butterflies to be featured on the invitations, on any order of service, in the decoration on the day and maybe even on the cake itself. It is the same with your sales copy. If you decide that you want your pizza leaflets to be red with green writing and your logo in the top right-hand corner, then that should be carried through the posters and on any other publicity material. The public are easily confused and, if you produce one design for your leaflets and another for the posters, they will not necessarily make the connection that this is the same company – worse still they may think it is for a rival pizza house and end up going there! I am sure you would not want to pay to advertise someone else's pizza place.

Remember this

To create a multiple sales strategy, ensure that every aspect complements and reinforces the message you want to give and keep to a uniform style and appearance.

Some truths about your customer

When writing sales copy we are always encouraged to focus on the customer, but how do you do that when they could be anyone? In these days of Internet sales, they could literally be from anywhere in the world, with different cultures and agendas. How on earth do you cope with such diversity?

The answer here is to concentrate not on their differences but on their similarities. Although we may indeed be very different, there are also lots of things that most people have in common and these offer us a wealth of opportunity for direction. Below is a list that you can begin to consider:

They are just like you – although people can appear quite different, in many ways we are similar and so, when looking to produce sales copy, look to yourself. What do you like? What do you think looks attractive or works well? The thing is that, if you like it, there is a good chance that others will like it too. That being said...

There will always be someone who does not like your style. You can't please everyone in any aspect of life. If anyone disagrees with your ideas, listen to their thoughts but if you still want the original design (and it is your business) – go with your instincts.

They like simplicity – keep the idea and design simple. There are many examples of simple design all around us and it can be far more powerful than clever links or complex ideas.

They like speed and want things fast – everybody wants things now. If you are reading this book on e-reading equipment, one of the reasons for choosing this method over a traditional book could have been the speed at which you could download it and immediately access the contents. People now want to access food, information, products and goods quickly and efficiently. We live in a world of 'I want it now' and, of course, the longer we have to wait, the more we will be tempted by other offers.

They like anything free – the current generation are used to receiving information free. Rather than buy into schemes offering access to advice or buying books, many people will now search the Internet for what advice, information and goods are available for free. An example of this is that many paper-based encyclopaedias have been phased out. There is so much information free that we do not need to pay for it. People therefore are beginning to expect something for nothing. The lesson here is to feature a deal or special offer, before your competitors do.

...but they want to know the value – put a monetary value on everything you are offering. This helps to persuade the person to make their choice. There are some things that have no exact monetary value, such as information or time; however, you must strive to calculate one. For example, '**These secrets of copywriting that I am ready to share with you have been learned over a 20-year period in sales and are worth over £100,000. That is 20 years of hard work that you can have in your hands RIGHT NOW for the simple price of...**' There is no way that you can really calculate the value of 20 years of experience and therefore the sum has been plucked from the air as a reasonable comparator to the offer price. In the buyer's mind, they are saving all that time and money and they get to download it right now – irresistible.

Reasonable prices sell goods – I recently saw a pack of six craft pens for sale and the offer included a free disk on how to use them as well as free postage and packing. I bought them because the price was low and the offer seemed reasonable enough. I did not look at how much each pen was individually or evaluate the deal because I 'felt' that overall this was a fair offer. I had no evidence for this, but bought it anyway – and so will your customers.

People like safety – no risk or a guarantee always takes away any final niggling doubts. If people are sure that they can get their money back, they are more likely to try and buy. The fact that so many people never claim, even if they are not happy, is not an issue at the point of purchase.

They are attracted by testimonials – testimonials enable the buyer to justify their sale. Usually, by the time the testimonials are read, the person has decided whether or not they are seriously interested. The testimonial just confirms that other people like them have also decided to buy that particular product or service and they think it is great. They address the

'Ah buts' that we discussed earlier in the book and enable the buyer to think 'well they liked it, so it must be good' and reassure themselves that this is a good purchase.

They trust people – we all like to think that we are speaking to experts, honest people and likeable people. Therefore, if the advertisement contains a quote from a doctor, a leading expert or someone we see on our TVs all the time, we trust them to be speaking the truth.

They respond to someone they know – the point above is great for large-scale sales copy but, at a more local level, it could be just as simple as the relationship. Perhaps you are well known in the area and therefore people trust you as a local person. Personal endorsements are marketing gold dust (especially when they are celebrities) but don't forget local themes such as 'Buy British' or 'Buy from Kent'.

Key idea

These are all broad aspects that most people buy into, no matter where they are from or what they are looking for. They are assumptions we can make. They are not all suitable for every occasion and therefore you need to pick and choose the most appropriate in each case.

Why you should be selling yourself

In the previous section I talked about using expert opinions and credible people to endorse your product, but there is someone else who can sell your product or service for you – YOU!

If you are writing sales copy for a company, then you may be able to hide behind the company name and reputation. However, if you are writing sales copy for your own business and aiming to sell your own services, then you need to consider your own credibility in the process and exercise the power that your own reputation can bring.

What does that mean? Well, whenever you start selling in your new business you will create a customer base of people who buy from you. You hope they stay loyal to you because that is the way to be efficient in business: it is far easier to maintain customers than to find new ones. As you progress, you may even get to know some of your customers quite well and they start to trust you. You are now moving towards something called Customer Relationship Management (CRM), which means you have a 'relationship' with the customer and this facilitates future sales. Suddenly it is the power of you that is driving sales: people want to do business with you because they like and respect you.

Do you remember the man who liked the shaver so much that he bought the business, or Colonel Sanders and his Kentucky Fried Chicken? Both used their own images and stories to sell their goods and create great copy. Is this something you have overlooked in your business? Could you be the figurehead of your own sales?

Even if you are not ready to plaster your picture all over your copy, perhaps you are able to give your own endorsement. Of course you can do this only if your product is credible, and of good quality, but, assuming that it is, you could create your own persuasive copy around your own interaction with your customers.

Remember this

Nobody knows your customers as well as you do and using your own reputation as persuasive copy really puts the seal on quality. It says to the customer that you are willing to put your own name to this and to be seen overtly recommending it – a winning combination.

Talk about the 'problem'

In producing sales copy, don't be afraid to talk about the problem. You can be direct:

> **Smelly feet?**
>
> **Boy do we have a great product for you – Nomorepong!**

Or more discreet:

> **I noticed something the other day that so many people seem to have a problem with. I was sitting in my lounge**

with my friend and wanted to take my shoes off, but I was too embarrassed, can you guess why? After a long walk in tight-fitting shoes I was worried about foot odour...

If you are addressing a medical or health issue, don't shy away from talking about the problem. In this capacity the reader is likening you to a friendly doctor and is looking for an answer to a difficult situation. They want to be assured of a friendly approach that seems to understand their problem. (Notice how the second example is written in the first person, as if the writer is confiding in the reader and asking them to empathize with their situation.)

Remember this

When you talk about the problem you can either spell it out directly (a shock tactic) or approach it indirectly, appearing to let the reader in on a private discussion.

Set out the benefits

Second to talking about the problem is our old friend: setting out the benefits. The reader will not always know all the benefits in your product and so you must spell them out clearly. Let's look at those two examples again:

> Smelly feet?
>
> Boy do we have a great product for you – Nomorepong!
>
> From now on...

► no more odour

► no more hiding shoes and slippers

► go barefoot without embarrassment.

Immediately as a potential purchaser I know exactly what this product is for and how I will benefit from using it.

Now let's look at the second example:

> I noticed something the other day that so many people seem to have a problem with. I was sitting in my lounge

with my friend and wanted to take my shoes off, but I was too embarrassed, can you guess why? After a long walk in tight-fitting shoes I was worried about foot odour. It is SO embarrassing but now I can take my shoes off whenever I want thanks to Nomorepong. Now my feet just don't smell, I don't have to hide my shoes and slippers from guests and I can even go barefoot.

Both sell the same benefits but in a different way. The first example is more suited to a newspaper or small ad, but the second would work well in a longer advertisement, taking up a full or half page, or even a short advertorial.

Key idea

In sales copy there is no need to be shy about going to the heart of the matter. State the issue and then set out the benefits so that the reader can fully understand them.

More techniques

Finally, here are some more techniques you may like to integrate into your work to help you to craft the perfect sales copy.

Get a killer headline – we are back to grabbing attention yet again. The more we can tickle the reader's interest, the better a position we will be in to deliver our message. You will be competing against some real experts in the field here, but don't be put off; channel your thoughts and ideas. You could:

▶ *Use an exciting verb*: Astound and Thrill Your Customer.

▶ *Adapt a song title*: We Gotta Get Outta This Place, If It's the Last Thing We Ever Do: for a flyer on career planning.

▶ *Adapt a film title*: The Good, The Bad and The Ugly – which one are you?

▶ *Use a pun*: Dieting – Don't Spend £s Losing Pounds.

▶ *Use a teasing question*: Why Don't Teachers Teach?

▶ *Be surprising*: Say Yes To More Work.

▶ *Be provocative*: Let's Go To War: for a flyer on recycling.

▶ *Show how to do something*: How would you like to be a millionaire?

▶ *Use an analogy or metaphor*: A Stitch in Time Saves Nine; for a flyer for a time management course.

▶ *Adapt a well-known concept*: Carrot or Stick: which would you rather use?

▶ **Use numbers** – readers love numbers. They love five ways to do something or the ten best things. They also love statistics such as 'Improve your life by 99.9%'.

▶ **Use 'You' as much as possible** – always keep it personal so that it feels to the reader that you are actually addressing them. For example 'Do you really want to change? Yes, I'm talking to you! Do you really want to change your life?'

▶ **Emphasize important words in bold or highlight** – don't be afraid to highlight certain words or embolden them. When we speak we vocally emphasize certain words within our sentences – these are the same words that you should be emphasizing in your writing.

Remember this

Standing out from the crowd is not easy, but, if you want your message to reach the maximum number of people, you need it to incorporate a few techniques to make sure your sales copy is noticed.

Focus points

Try using the AIDA formula with your sales copy.

Consider creating a multiple sales strategy so that you strengthen your brand and maximize sales opportunities. However, ensure that all aspects of the strategy complement each other.

There are some general truths about customers that we need to be aware of and then use this information to build our sales copy.

You are a fantastic reason for anyone to buy your products. Make sure you are credible and then use your own charisma to generate sales.

There is no need to shy away from the problem. Just make sure that you are able to offer practical and winning solutions with your product.

Case studies

Let's see how Leonie and Paul put this information to use.

The personnel officer was delighted with Leonie's efforts and offers her a job in the sales team for a trial period of three months. Leonie is very excited but also nervous. She desperately wants to impress but realizes that this is all very new to her and so she should not rush things. She decides that, as this is a trial, she will not tell her friends about her new job until it is confirmed. On the first morning she turns up for work and, after the initial introductions and a tour of the offices, she is set a task. The manager asks Leonie to come up with some ideas for a short high-impact advertisement for a new shoe manufacturer that makes children's and ladies' shoes. The team just need some more ideas to pad out the couple they already have placed in their presentation. Leonie looks back through this book and comes up with the idea of a series of three photos of shoes, each with a different strap line. The first is a pair of children's shoes and the line is 'Tough on scuffs', the second a pair of ladies' high heels and the line 'Deals in heels' and the last one a pair of comfy shoes with the line 'Shoes with sole'. Her ideas are entered in with the others and discussed with the customer. Leonie is delighted to be told that the customer loved her advertisement campaign so much that they have decided to go with that one.

Paul bowls Mr Pan over with his ideas. When he reflects on the situation he is pleased that he devoted so much time to planning the meeting; it enabled him to deliver his message carefully and with due regard to Mr Pan's feelings. It was a great idea that Paul planned his approach to Mr Pan as if he were selling, because that is exactly what it was – selling his idea. However, Mr Pan surprises Paul with his request that the campaign start as soon as possible if it is to meet all the ideas in his proposal. Mr Pan has also warmed considerably to 'Haulage with Heart' and is thinking of having it painted on all his vehicles and so what started out as an idea for business growth is suddenly becoming part of Pan Haulage's future sales strategy. Mr Pan shares with Paul that he believes that the future for the next ten years lies in creating a strong alliance with family values and he asks Paul to come up with more ideas about how Pan Haulage can reach out to the community and build on this idea. He loves the idea of being featured in the newspaper as he believes that many local people do not know the full extent of how Pan Haulage can help them; they think of it as a business that works only with major companies and retailers. Paul suddenly realizes that he is now in the position of creating a multiple sales strategy that could meet all their goals and decides to give the whole idea more considered thought. If he is going down this route he needs to think about consistency, style, colours and logo. It is very exciting.

Next step

In this chapter we have looked at the role of persuasive writing in sales copy. Sales copy is a fact of life in any business and it is a useful skill to be able to produce effective sales copy. By using certain techniques anyone can produce wining lines that will have a great effect on your sales. In the next chapter we will be taking these ideas one step forward and considering how persuasive writing can be used for websites and web-based advertising.

9

Using Persuasive Techniques on the Web

Goal – to demonstrate how many of the techniques given may be applied to blogs and websites.

Diagnostic test

Answer each question by choosing a number from 1 to 5. Nearer to 1 indicates that you feel this statement to be *false or incorrect* and nearer to 5 indicates that you feel it is *more likely to be true*.

I use the Internet for most of my research and information gathering

I believe that most businesses now have a website

I think having a web 'presence' is a good thing

I feel confident producing copy for the Internet

I understand that copy for the Internet is different in many respects

I think that there are sometimes more opportunities to be influential through a website

I recognize that some web pages are more successful than others

I think that writing copy for a website or blog can be fun

I believe that anyone can produce useful and enjoyable web-based copy

I believe that Internet sales is a growing market

Now add up your score and see what it says about you.

Result

35–50   This score indicates that you not only use the Internet frequently but also feel comfortable and able to produce copy that can be displayed on a site. You recognize that businesses increasingly need more copy for their websites, as many sites need a complete refresh every two or three years. This results in plenty of work for those who are good at producing persuasive writing for the Internet. However, even though you feel comfortable with using this medium, you may not have considered the many aspects of actually writing for online sites. Read through the chapter and remind yourself of the techniques you can use. The results will be improved copy and a renewed appreciation for its applications.

20–34 This score indicates that you may be using the Internet to access goods and personal items but have not actually thought of writing copy specifically aimed at websites or recognized that different techniques are used. Writing copy for the web can be hugely satisfying and rewarding, but it needs specific techniques to be taken into consideration if you are to make a sizeable difference to sales or persuade the reader to take action. This chapter will equip you with those skills, which you can then put into operation in whatever field you are working in. The result will be a greater response rate and more reader satisfaction.

Below 20 Your lower score here indicates that you either do not use the Internet or have not spotted its potential for your writing. The number of Internet sites is increasing every day and they all need an inexhaustible supply of persuasive copy. Not only that but you may want to have your own website to market your business and that will need updating and renewing periodically. Finally, persuasive copy does not have to be only for your website; it can be a blog or even the descriptions you enter into online auctions or advertising sites. Go ahead and read this chapter – there is great potential for everyone to produce more persuasive copy in any medium.

You would have had to have been on another planet not to appreciate the impact that the Internet has had on our lives. The last decade has seen unparalleled development that has literally changed the way we do business, have hobbies, integrate socially and run our lives.

Remember this

Make a quick note of all the functions that you undertake over the internet. Do you use it for shopping? Communicating with friends? Sharing photographs? What else?

Most people use the Internet every day of their lives. They use it for pleasure and for business and it has become an integral part of the way we operate. Even mobile phones are now mini computers that allow us to browse and download data from the Internet on the go. In fact we never seem to be away from its influences. But have you ever thought that writing web content is different in nature and therefore requires its own approach? This chapter will provide you with the tools to integrate your persuasive writing into this new medium.

Structuring and chunking

In the past, most people who needed information would have turned to a book to find out what they needed to know.

Remember this

Pick up a book (if there is one nearby). Look at the covers, flick through the pages and describe in what ways it is different from information you may find on the Internet.

Some of the things you may have noticed include:

Books	Websites
You can look at the cover and assess the content	Websites do not always give you the full details of their content
By looking at the size of the book you know exactly how large it is	You don't really get an idea of how large a website is as you cannot see the subpages
A book is a definitive object in itself, a complete unit	Websites link to other websites and become a sprawling mass of inter-relating information
Most of the text in a book is free-flowing, not in boxes or sections other than the original chapters	All information is in boxes and chunks. There may be side advertisements and links to other sites
You can make notes on the pages	You cannot write on a website
You can fold the corner down to mark a page and return to exactly that spot whenever you wish	Although you can bookmark your favourite sites, the content of that page may have changed (or the page may even have been withdrawn) by the time you recall it
You tend to read a book in the order in which it is presented	Websites are accessed in a range of orders and you may not even access it from the home page
There is often a chapter list at the front and an index at the back of the book	Although some websites have a search function it is not always fully effective

I am sure you recognized other differences too. Books are designed to be held, transported, picked up and put down, whereas websites are designed to be read in one sitting, in easy, truncated blocks of text, and direct the reader to another site if necessary. Quite simply, you may invest a significant amount of money in a book but give a website hardly a minute of your time. In fact, if the site is too difficult to access or find your way around, the likelihood is that the reader will give up and go to another site.

So here is our first lesson: when writing persuasive copy for a website you need to consider structure. You can do this through asking yourself (or your customer) some questions such as:

▶ What is the website there to achieve?

▶ How do you want the reader to move through the website?

▶ What is the ultimate goal of the reader?

▶ What action do we want the reader to take?

From these questions you can start to draw a box structure or flow diagram on a piece of paper to create a map that shows the ideal path of the reader. There can be various offshoots where they may go down another level onto a subpage, but we need to persuade them back up again, so that we, the writer, can guide them through to the conclusion.

When we have our map of the site we can then consider what information will be featured on each webpage. This is where chunking comes in.

Not everyone scrolls down the webpage and therefore it is essential not to make the page too long. Ideally the page should be only as long as is comfortably visible on a monitor. The reader will also read in small sections and therefore the message you need to convey must be chunked up into small easy 'bites' of information: no rambling passages or detailed paragraphs. We will look at this issue in more depth later but, for now, think about keeping your persuasive copy short and tight.

The point size and font design will also need to be reasonable for comfortable reading, as monitors do not make the most comfortable reading platforms. There should also be no repetition. Each page should hold some new information that connects and leads the reader to the desired result.

How visitors scan pages

In the same way that you may scan your TV for programmes, flicking from one channel to the next with the remote control, that is how readers (or visitors to sites) scan through websites. If your site is not immediately appealing, they will scan onwards, leaving your website behind, and therefore it is not sufficient to simply attract attention; you will need to hold their attention.

In 2002, a study observed over 40 people while they read online news sites. They found a number of interesting points. The research indicated that initially readers started in the upper left-hand corner, moved from left to right and then went to the bottom of the page before returning up to the right-hand column. There was also evidence that smaller type encouraged careful reading whereas larger type appeared to encourage scanning. Other findings were that stories displayed in a single column received more attention than those split into two or more columns, and short paragraphs received more attention than long paragraphs.

There has been further study and it is now reported that many readers follow an 'F-shaped' reading pattern. Readers would start at the top left again, scan straight across, then drop down and scan across to the right again. Finally they would scan the left side by going straight down.

Key idea

These findings back up what most writers and journalists know: that we need to pay more attention to the start and end of our features as that is where the attention lies.

As writers of persuasive text, we can use this information to target our message so that it packs a punch in these two hot spots.

Earlier in this chapter we looked at the difference between a book and a website. This is hugely important when trying to catch visitor's attention because when you write a book you write it for many people and you hope to engage in some way with the reader. However, the website visitor is looking for more from a website: they are looking for a relationship with the site. They are looking for a site that appeals to them, reaches out and speaks directly to them, using their language. There is a lot of competition and your website visitor will simply move on if they do not think your site is for them.

Hooks and page links

I have talked about hooks earlier. They are the enticing words that instantly 'hook' the reader into wanting to know more. In all kinds of writing they are important but there the similarity ends. In a book your hook could be the first sentence, paragraph or even the first page. On a website you don't have this luxury and the hook must be instant – within the first few words. In a book you may be leading or enticing the reader, but on a website the hook might be the bold description of the site; for example, Biggest Water Park in Britain or Fishing in The Lakes. You might think, well, those don't exactly sound like well-crafted and lovingly honed hooks, they sound a bit too bold to entice and tantalize the reader. Correct! That is because no one looks on a website and gives you enough air time to be drawn in. They will use a search engine to look for the biggest water park in Britain or where to fish in The Lakes and want to know that the site that comes up is exactly what they want. Therefore you are not only satisfying the reader, reassuring them that they have selected the correct site, but also writing to satisfy the search engine. (For the search engine to pick up 'fishing The Lakes' it will have to have those exact words in a prominent place on your site).

If we follow the advice in the last section we need to be careful where we place these hooks for maximum effect. You can use your more tantalizing text further down in the main section.

Key idea

The idea of a hook here is slightly different from that in our usual text. However, it is still a hook to encourage the visitor to the site to stay with us and read on.

Now let's think about links. Links are the words that sometimes appear in bold and/or underlined and indicate to the visitor that they can click on them to be taken to another page or even another site. They can be obvious, for example:

Click here

or part of a sentence, such as:

...and when you visit the Plaza you must take in **Betsy's Tea Rooms** for a fantastic cream tea.

When the visitor to the site places their cursor over **Betsy's Tea Rooms** the cursor will change and a message will appear, to show that this is a link to somewhere, perhaps another page with a map or menu, or maybe even Betsy's own website.

A good link should have a hook (again) and some blurb surrounding it to tell the visitor what it is for. For example:

Click here for information on cream teas

Click here for directions to Betsy's Team rooms

This is particularly important if you want to present your reader with a simple list of links, rather than a long narrative.

To encourage the visitor to click on the link you can phrase the blurb in a range of different ways. For example:

▶ *Use quotation marks* – for credibility.

'We love going to Betsy's' Click here to find out more...

▶ *Design a question* – that will leave the visitor wanting an answer.

Want to find out who bakes the best scones in the world? Click here

▶ *Create an unusual statement* – to surprise and jolt your reader.

Plaza, my foot! You want to be here {click me}

▶ *Create a comparison or contrast* – compare similarities or contrast differences.

Other cake shops are good but we are world class – find out more here

▶ *Highlight a news item* – tie your link in with any current news.

News flash! Cakes win prizes – find out more

▶ *The promise of gossip* – everyone will want to find out more.

You simply won't believe this... – click here

All of these are designed to tantalize the reader into clicking on the link, allowing us, the writer, to direct them as we wish. Some of these links may simply take the reader to another page of our own website where even more persuasive writing is awaiting them.

Remember this

If we want the reader to go to a specific page, we need to make it interesting or tantalizing for them to go there and also make the job of getting there as easy as possible. If your link goes to a dead page, the visitor may just give up. On the Internet, the reader's attention span is short.

Cut, rethink, cut, rethink

Now we have our reader at the page where we hold the longer message. It is vital that as writers we constantly cut and rethink our text to make it better and tighter. Let's look at an example below:

> Welcome to the site for Llanadoch Castle, nestling in the hills of Llanadochshire. The castle has been in existence since Medieval times and has improved and extended ever since. Now it is a castle of fine character sat in around 100 acres of forests and fine lands. Today the owner is the 8th Earl of Llanadoch and his family. He succeeded the title from his father in 1980. The family still live in the castle and help out with many of the functions (you may even see Lady Llanadoch serving tea!)
>
> While at the castle you can feast on venison in our open rotisserie and also try some jousting and falconry. There is a maze for the children and a bar for adults. Although we have many family days out, we can also house corporate events and weddings. There are even six bedrooms where guests can stay.
>
> If you want to come to a see a castle that is brimming with excitement, come to Llanadoch Castle today.

There is nothing fundamentally wrong with this text and you will see similar information on many sites on the Internet. That is the problem. In a contest against another site would it win your vote? Would it persuade you?

The first point I would like to note is that just about everything is in here, all jumbled together. Corporate events and weddings vie with family days out – and all on the home page. Time for some trimming, methinks.

The first paragraph consists of a welcome followed by a description and some history. Personally I would move the history to a separate page and add a link. That leaves us with:

> Welcome to the site for Llanadoch Castle, nestling in the hills of Llanadochshire.

While at the castle you can feast on venison in our open rotisserie and also try some jousting and falconry. There is a maze for the children and a bar for adults. Although we have many family days out, we can also house corporate events and weddings. There are even six bedrooms where guests can stay.

If you want to come to a see a castle that is brimming with excitement, come to Llanadoch Castle today.

Now let's turn our attention to the second paragraph. This has so much in it, you almost miss the detail, so how about putting that information in a bulleted list, like this?

Welcome to the site for Llanadoch Castle, nestling in the hills of Llanadochshire.

While at the castle you can:

▶ feast on venison

▶ try jousting and falconry

▶ explore the maze

▶ hang out in our bar and cafe.

If you are interested in either a wedding in Llanadoch Castle or a corporate event click here for details.

If you want to come to a see a castle that is brimming with excitement, come to Llanadoch Castle today.

That is better and far more punchy. However, I think we need one more rewrite. How about?

Welcome to Llanadoch Castle!!

The finest medieval castle nestling in the hills of Llanadochshire.

Join us today to:

▶ feast on venison

▶ try jousting and falconry

▶ explore the maze

▶ hang out in our bar and cafe.

Enjoy a day out in a real castle brimming with excitement and history.

Visit us today!

If you are interested in either a wedding in Llanadoch Castle or a corporate event click here for details.

What do you think? Do you think it looks better shorter and with links? Would you want to visit? I think so, but of course we all have different tastes and that is what makes writing such an interesting subject. If you disagree, feel free to work on the words further.

Key idea

Don't be afraid to write, cut, rewrite and rework until your work starts to look more interesting and persuasive.

Blogs

The strength of growth in weblogs (or blogs) has caught many people unprepared and has been one of the most interesting developments since the Internet has evolved. Suddenly it was not only easy to produce a credible site without any prior knowledge, it also gave an interface with which to communicate regularly with readers and customers, even updating them several times a day. The Internet immediately became fluid and, rather than asking a company to create a website for you that then you could not change and so it sat there for at least a year, you could create for yourself an interactive site that you could change on the go, even updating it on your way to work.

Blogs tend to be more personal and you are just as likely to find a blog on knitting as you are on a business subject. There may also be blogs given over to subjects such as the World Cup, or blogs detailing personal issues such as life in our street, or someone's search for a job. However, never underestimate the power of a well-written blog. They may appear to be written by amateurs but their effortless friendliness can hide some very professional writing! Some blogs have even made celebrities and future authors of their writers, as publishing houses now scour them for talent and ideas.

When you blog, you don't just update a section on a page (as you might on a website); you post new information and so the person receiving the post will expect a whole new page. If the reader is new to the blog they can usually scroll down to see previous posts to enable them to catch up and feel up to date with the 'conversation'. Each posting is like a new page and they don't link together in the same way as a website, with pages off other pages. Each post then needs to be carefully considered as a unit in its own right. It needs an attention-grabbing hook, excellent and interesting prose (with pictures if you can) and a neat closer that sounds personal and friendly. The golden rule here is to keep it fairly short (and if you need to put in something longer, like a presentation or a video, put it in a PDF or podcast and provide a link).

Although blogs seem effortless, if you are writing them on behalf of someone else (acting as ghost writer for a celebrity, perhaps) who is simply too busy, you will be under pressure to ensure that the content is right. That means no gaffes and no typos. It may look like a note to a friend, but actually it is a highly polished piece of persuasive copy.

Blogs are intended to be interactive, so don't be surprised if other readers respond to your writing. It is great that they feel able to contact you and that is how you get into a relationship with your readers. Once your readers are in step with you, you can lead them with your suggestions through the use of further persuasive writing. Blogging may seem like fun, and in some cases it is, but for many it is actually big business.

Remember this

Professional bloggers carefully manage the messages they send out to their readers. They recognize the impact they have on others and the persuasive possibilities that can arise from blogging. Although blogging can appear light hearted and frivolous, it can also send serious messages.

E-zines

E-zines are online magazines. The great thing about e-zines is that they are produced regularly and need a constant intake of information to stay current. That means that they are a great opportunity for the persuasive writer.

E-zine features are written very much like those for a magazine except that they are shorter, because the reader is having to access them on a screen, and can hold links to other sites. This enables the reader to interact with the material in a different way. If they like what they are reading they can click on a link to go directly to further information. This enables the e-zine writer to shorten their features; they don't have to give any long explanations. For example, if you wanted to discuss the merits of a car, you could give your opinion and the link (so that the reader could go to the site to look at the car itself), which saves the e-zine writer many words and maybe even the need to produce pictures.

E-zines are growing in popularity because there are more handheld devices available now and because they are easy to transport and store. They can be quicker to read and download instantly – making the reader feel very much in control of the process.

Key idea

E-zines can be a real boost to a business as its information can go out wide and be in your customer's mail box in an instant. Writing persuasively for e-zines is a sought-after skill and could get you recognized.

Focus points

Websites are very different from written copy. They work by a different set of rules and visitors read them in a different way.

Start to tackle your text by considering the structure of the site and chunking up your text.

Don't forget to add in hooks and links. They can vitalize your page and also allow you to put vast amounts of text on another page where only someone interested in that data will access it.

Keep cutting and rethinking your text until you feel that it is right. Remember that you will never get to a point where everyone thinks it is spot on – just aim to please your customer.

Blogging and writing for e-zines are a great way of reaching out to the public and can be highly persuasive. However, craft your messages with care, as this can be a very powerful medium.

Case studies

Let's see how Leonie and Paul are getting on with their organizations.

Hot on the back of Leonie's suggestions for the shoe advertisement campaign being accepted by the customer, they ask the company if they would like to start a professionally run blog to accompany the adverts. Leonie is shocked when her manager suggests that she might like to write for the blog. She has only been there for two weeks and everything is moving too fast. She is very unsure, but her manager encourages her by telling Leonie how much faith she has in her and that she would happily read every blog before it went out to check it over and make sure Leonie's writing is acceptable. Leonie accepts but notices a negotiating opportunity here. She knows that the company will get more money for the blog and so she says that she will do it on the understanding that, after being there for six months, she can be put forward for some professional training – because she believes she has finally found the right job for her. Leonie's manager is pleased that she is taking the job seriously. The company is growing and her department will be expanding; she needs staff such as Leonie to stay around and take on some of the more tricky jobs and it seems only fair that she should be trained. Leonie has made an excellent start and begins to plan the blog site with the IT expert at work.

Mr Pan seems to be in such an accommodating mood that Paul decides to take his multiple sales strategy one step further. The company has a website but it is only one page and rather flat and boring. No one updates it or enters any new information and it is verging on looking out of date.

Paul approaches Mr Pan about whether he could take it over. Mr Pan is delighted and explains that he had it made years ago but has never had any more to do with it because, as he explained, "IT is a bit nerve racking and I wanted to concentrate on the business." Paul explains to Mr Pan that it is all very different now and that he would be able to produce a website that would actually encourage business and might even generate 'followers'. Mr Pan is not too worried and tells Paul to just make sure that anything is seen by him before it goes on line. Paul agrees with this and sets about structuring a site that not only gives the reader information about the company but also their future plans, the 'Haulage with Heart' campaign, a new section *and* a 'Fans of Pan' blog encouraging people to spot Pan's Haulage vehicles on the road. Mr Pan is astonished by the end result; it is well thought out and much more than he thought. Paul asks him for two hours of his work time every week to be devoted to its upkeep and Mr Pan agrees. On the day they launch the site Mr Pan is amazed to find that, after only one day, there are already 20 'Fans of Pan' who have registered their interest. Maybe he should have thought about this before and for the first time begins to think of how Pan's Haulage could expand even further. Paul is persuading Mr Pan by taking a very slow route. Mr Pan is also building his trust in Paul and believing in his ideas.

Next step

In this chapter we have looked at how websites and blogs can, through the use of persuasive writing, reach out to customers and create new and interesting relationships upon which you can build. Websites and e-zines need a constant stream of well-written material and therefore they are an excellent source of business for the persuasive writer. In the next chapter we will be looking at the persuasive writer at work and how these skills can be used in a business setting.

10

Using Persuasive Techniques at Work

Goal – to explore techniques that will increase your returns and increase your chance of success at work.

Diagnostic test

Answer each question by choosing a number from 1 to 5. Nearer to 1 indicates that you feel this statement to be *false or incorrect* and nearer to 5 indicates that you feel it is *more likely to be true*.

I already use persuasive writing at work

I understand how writing persuasively can benefit my work

I think everyone can develop how they use persuasive writing at work

I feel totally confident about producing persuasive copy in a work setting

I am clear that writing persuasively can help my career and the future of the business

I believe we can all use these techniques

I recognize that sometimes it is easier to write persuasively than at other times

I believe that writing persuasively at work can be good for my career

I think that well-written persuasive writing can be unobtrusive

I believe that persuasive writing at work can help projects to happen

Now add up your score and see what it says about you.

Result

35–50   This score indicates that you probably already use persuasive techniques at work. You are right in that they can help both business to move forwards at a pace and your career to flourish. People love positivity; when you take the lead and persuade someone at work that your idea is sound, you take them with you and your work will appear to move forwards at a pace, with everyone agreeing with you. I am sure you have heard of the expression 'a self-fulfilling prophecy' – well that is what happens when one person is positive about their work and persuades everyone else to be too. It just becomes a success because how can it not be? However, you may be interested in this chapter to see how the techniques for persuasive writing can be broken down into their different applications and you may still pick up some tips along the way.

20–34   This score indicates that you may not be completely sure whether you are using persuasive techniques or you are trying but not feeling very successful. Writing persuasively is a skill and, like all skills, it takes time to learn and use proficiently. In this chapter we will be looking at specific applications for persuasive writing that you can use at work. To begin with, use these with a light hand until you feel capable and confident enough to push the boundaries a little further. Persuasive writing is not just about getting things done; everything you write says something about you and so your persuasive writing will also inform others of your own skills. You may find that your career benefits as a result!

Below 20   Your lower score here indicates that either you do not use persuasive writing in a business situation or you still lack confidence in this area. All skills take time to learn and in this book I have taken you through at a pace. You need time to develop these skills and apply them to your own working environment. Persuasive writing is not only for sales situations. There will be times when you also want to persuade someone to allow something, for example agree to some leave, and you want to present it in a way that is more acceptable to the recipient. It cannot guarantee that you will get what you want but it will guarantee you a better chance of success than had you not used it. Read through this chapter and then see how these applications can help you in your work.

Up to this point in this book we have been looking at techniques and specific aspects of persuasive writing. In this chapter I want us to consider how a typical person can integrate persuasive writing into their day-to-day work. This means not picking it out as a specialism of sales or website writing, but just how any employee can use the techniques of persuasive writing to increase their chances of being acknowledged as a professional, furthering the projects that they are looking after and persuading others to come on board with their ideas. Everyone has the opportunity to try out these techniques in the workplace and you just might find out that the results are not only about the work!

Remember this

Think for one moment. What are the functional activities at work in which you could integrate some form of persuasive writing? Are you already flexing your persuasive muscles without recognizing it? What more could you do?

You may have thought of quite a few tasks in which you could use persuasive writing, but in this chapter we will be looking at:

► business planning

► appraisal paperwork

► writing letters

► creating presentations

► general reports

► crafting newsletters

all of which can benefit from some persuasive writing magic dust.

Writing a killer business plan

A business plan has two main functions:

► it shows the outside world (shareholders, banks and so forth) what your business intends to do

► it is a planning tool for employees within the business.

Businesses are intended to grow. That means that the business plan must show growth or the planning of movement into new areas where future growth is possible. Business growth is based on a number of factors, but one of them is that people should have faith in the business. Indeed, businesses in the past have been 'talked up' and the shares sold out, before they have even proven themselves in their market. This happened many times with the early 'dot com' companies, which had yet to prove that they would survive in the new and untried world of online shopping. Unfortunately this has led to mistrust and investors are now far more wary of overnight successes and fast growth. Therefore, what everyone is looking for is prolonged, steady growth.

Everyone needs to have faith in the business, including the bank, from which your company may have borrowed money, and any private investors. Of course the converse is also true: if no one has anything good to say about a company, the staff will become disenchanted and leave and the company will cease to attract customers. Honesty within the realms of positivity is therefore vital for all aspects of your business and it is here that the power of persuasive writing can help.

Remember this

Find your company or team business plan and look at the way in which it is written. Certain aspects (such as the financial figures) will be presented in a formulaic way, so ignore them for now and instead concentrate on reading the remaining copy. How positive is the copy? Do you feel that this represents a growing business?

Let's look at an example of what I mean:

Your business plan could read:

> In the first quarter of the year we were able to cover our costs and raised our assets by 30 per cent. This level of savings was required because we foresaw a fall in profits in the second quarter of the year. This will be due to the lack of tourism opportunities during the second quarter, which would have boosted sales. It is to be hoped that this is improved upon in the third quarter, as this will have an effect on our overall profits for the year.

Or it could read:

> We had an excellent first quarter in which we not only
> covered our costs but also, through judicious planning and
> excellent negotiation, increased our assets by 30 per cent – a
> huge bonus, for which we extend our thanks to the staff
> and all our stakeholders. We foresee a more challenging
> environment during the second quarter but we are putting
> plans in place to ensure that any downturn is recouped
> during the third quarter, thereby leaving us still ahead of
> our predictions for the year thus far.

Which one could I persuade you to invest in?

Personally, I prefer the second example. There is nothing
fundamentally wrong with the first example – it is factual and
many business plans are just like this – but it could raise alarm
regarding the second quarter (indeed perhaps that is what the
writer intended). In the second example there is more of an attempt
to contain any panic, smoothing over certain factors and thanking
people. There is more of a friendly message between the lines about
how we do business that is more likely to attract others and it
does not dwell on the negative (any reader who wishes to delve
deeper will be able to see the facts from the figures).

Key idea

Business plans do not have to be simple fact; they can be embellished
and made more motivational. Many business relations are hinged on
perception and therefore positivity should be promoted.

Appraisal and performance

Appraisals are end of year assessments of your work and there
may also be a review appraisal partway through the year too.
I guess there is no problem with giving people good news; the
problems develop when we have to deliver the news that we
need the individual staff member to improve their performance.
It is then crucial that good quality targets are written so that
staff can work towards achieving them and everyone is clear
on what is required. The most commonly recommended way
of setting targets is to apply the mnemonic **SMART**, which

we have seen before, earlier in this book. If you remember, the mnemonic stands for:

- ▶ **S** – specific: they must be detailed
- ▶ **M** – measurable: so that they can be monitored
- ▶ **A** – agreed: that is agreed with the manager and the individual
- ▶ **R** – realistic: so that they can be achieved
- ▶ **T** – timed: so that resources can be set and again they can be measured.

In Chapter 3, I used them to describe how to set goals that have every aspect included and here we are using the mnemonic to set targets in appraisals.

However, I would like to add one more item to that list. That is another 'M' because I believe they should be motivational. If targets are not motivational, the person will be less inclined to do them. We can make performance improvement targets motivational by using persuasive language.

I am a great believer in explaining targets in detail. I believe that, if people understand the background to a situation and know exactly what they need to do to satisfy the targets, they are more likely to achieve them. We are also back to selling the benefits again, a theme we first met in Chapter 4. Let's look at an example.

I might have a target of:

> **To lose one stone in weight in the next six months.**

As long as I agree to this I would argue that it is **SMART** but it is not very motivational or inspirational, especially if someone else is telling me to do it. How about:

> **To lose one stone in weight in the next six months so that I can reward my efforts by buying a designer outfit to wear to my sister's wedding.**

or

> **To lose one stone in weight in the next six months so that I feel more healthy and can take up roller skating.**

Both of these examples provide not only a SMART target but also spell out the benefit to me of my reaching that target – and that will be my motivation.

Remember this

Have a look at your own business targets. Do they motivate you to make the changes required or are they quite flat? How could you make them more motivating?

I am not suggesting that you include weight loss targets in your business; it is just a light-hearted illustration of how we can increase the probability of reaching a target, by adding just a few more motivational words. Motivation is not something that anyone else can provide by force; it needs to come from you. I hope that, having read this far, you are motivated to continue and finish the book. Hopefully no one set it as a target for you, but you may want to explore in your own mind where that motivation came from.

Appraisal and target setting can be much more pleasant when we can persuade others to work towards their targets and help them find the motivation to succeed.

Letters and emails

Every organization has to produce letters and emails. Some of them will be instigating requests and others will be answering requests. Your company may even have templates for letter writing in an effort to make the responses more formalized, but even these letters need a second look from time to time.

The issue is: how do you want the person reading the letter to respond? If you want them to take some action, you need to work that into the letter and make it very clear. For example:

> **Upon receipt of this letter it would facilitate the process if you are able to respond with the appropriate documents (listed below) as soon as possible. I have enclosed an envelope to help with this.**

Or:

> Please send the documents listed below, today, in the enclosed envelope. As soon as we receive the documents we will be able to process your claim.

OK, so the first paragraph is somewhat flowery and overly formal but the point here is that many people would have put that letter down and then probably thought about it several times before getting around to sending the documents. If you want someone to act immediately, tell them so and then give them a reason to do so (their motivation). The sentence, 'As soon as we receive the documents we will be able to process your claim' is the motivator – the enticer to ensure they do as you ask.

Emails are somewhat different. There is something about an email that is rather casual compared with a letter. Even if you did put the letter down it is still there, in hard copy, at the side – whereas it is easy to forget an email, lose it or even delete it by mistake. Therefore, unless you want to reach out to a huge population at the hit of a button and do not mind if very few people respond – write a letter.

Key idea

Sales letters will often say 'Act immediately for a 10% reduction' or 'Send this off today to receive your free gift.' The reason they do this is because they know that, once the customer puts the letter down, they may not pick it up again and therefore they need to stimulate instant activity to ensure that sale. It is a similar story with emails. They will usually say 'Only available today' or 'Next 24 hours' because they know that, once it disappears into the mass called your inbox, it may be lost forever.

Presentations

Presentations have the added advantage of two additional factors:

▶ the use of graphics or images

▶ the opportunity to use yourself (voice and body) to provide additional material and credibility.

Pictures can enhance your words and sell a dream. For example, if you want to persuade your organization to invest in an overseas aid project, you need have very few words on your slides; just some photographs or film footage of the situation you are trying to help will speak volumes. Therefore, select your graphics wisely so that they convey exactly what you want to portray *and* provoke the reaction (or action) you are hoping to trigger.

Unless your presentation is a rolling slide show only, you will be there to deliver your message personally. Therefore, ensure that you portray not only the image that fits your message but also confidence. When you are in a presentation setting, those watching are automatically thrown into a teacher/pupil-type scenario. All attention is on you and, to command the attention of the group, you will need to be confident in your material and the way in which you deliver it. Their impression of you is just as important as your message.

Remember this

When you are present, sell yourself before anyone sees the message. The first few minutes are crucial for presenting yourself credibly to your audience and they may either buy into the presentation message or not, simply based on you.

If you are delivering a presentation to persuade someone to take some action, practise, practise, practise. Deliver verbally in the same way as you would if you were writing the whole presentation out in a letter. Re-read the techniques found in Chapter 4 and weave them into your presentation. Use metaphors and tell stories, build in repetition, show quotes and select figures that back up your message. Write this all out before practising your delivery. Ask yourself:

▶ Where can I ask a teasing question?

▶ At what point can I flatter my audience?

▶ Can I pause at any point to provide effect?

▶ Which messages can I emphasize with my voice or body movement?

▶ How is it best to deliver that final call to action?

You will find that all the best 'off the cuff' stand-up comedians have practised their material and delivery hundreds of times. Every nuance, every pause, is practised. There is no such thing as an successful unpractised, off-the-cuff presentation.

Key idea

Always complete your presentation with a slide designed to prompt immediate action. Tell the audience what you want them to do, so that this is the message they are left with, for example, 'Text now on XXX to make a donation' or 'Raise your hand now if you think this is a good idea' or 'Complete the slip in front of you to make an instant commitment to this idea'. Deliver it with conviction and you will find that your audience will comply with your request.

Reports

Reports are often described as the bugbear of many managers because usually they have to be written on a regular basis to evaluate a project, process or procedure and it just seems like a 'have to do' function rather than a 'good to do' function of the job. However, if you view them differently, you may start to see that there is a wealth of opportunity to persuade in every report and that makes them just that bit more interesting.

The nature of a report is that you are indeed reporting back, but that does not mean that there is no room for poetic licence to follow your findings with a conclusion and way forward that really packs a punch.

Let's look at this in more detail.

The introduction – here rather than simply stating facts you can introduce motivators that begin to prime your reader. For example instead of writing:

Example 1

Introduction

This report details the progress made for the first quarter on the channel production line. Following months of wrangling, the channel production line was secured on

21 January and work commenced on 23 February. All staff identified from the specification to begin chapter one were drafted into the project to begin work on 1 March.

You could write:

Example 2

Introduction

This report details the progress made for the first quarter on the much-awaited channel production line.

Following complex discussions, the contract for the channel production line was secured on 21 January. We were delighted that work could commence on 23 February as this exceeded our expectations and has impacted favourably on the business plan. Further, all staff identified from the original specification were still available and therefore their professional roles on this project started on 1 March, ahead of schedule.

Notice the difference between the two examples. Once again there is nothing wrong with the first example; it is just very factual. The second example shows how you can inject a little more personality into the report and, because you can tell that the writer is pleased with the progress, it is transmitted through the text and the reader will also feed pleased – which is good because later in the same report example 1 has some difficult news to give.

Example 1

Forecasting for the second quarter

Regrettably there is one problem on the horizon. Due to some unforeseen hitch, the land between Upminster and Downminster has not been cleared sufficiently for the line to be taken through and this could cause a delay during the second quarter.

The way that this is written, I would suggest, would cause alarm in the recipient and they may be worried that overall delivery of the project is threatened. Although factually correct, raising the alarm or losing customer confidence can be very damaging in business. Consider the following instead:

Example 2

> **Forecasting for the second quarter**

> **In looking forward, the project team believe that there are a number of issues that will need clarification. The most immediate is the land between Upminster and Downminster. Although it has not been cleared to our expectation as yet, I will be speaking to the developers tomorrow and hope to have the situation rectified before the second quarter so that it falls back in line with the original project plan.**

Can you see that the second example still lets the board know about the issue of the land but does not cause as much alarm in the reader? Projects can be disrupted and irrevocably damaged if stakeholders lose confidence in the team delivering the outcome. They may even cancel the project. Instead this second example aims to raise the point but it also inspires confidence that everything will be dealt with and the project will soon be back on track. Notice that the second example does not promise any specific outcome, but it feels more as if the project manager and team have the situation in hand.

Remember this

Although reports are there to provide information, they also offer you, the persuasive writer, an excellent opportunity to improve your own credibility and that of the team. Business runs on confidence and perception and you have to be a master at portraying both.

Newsletters

There are basically two types of newsletter that you may be asked to provide input for: external and internal.

External newsletters are sent to customers and stakeholders outside the organization. They may feature a little about staff successes but they mainly focus on new products and initiatives and success of the overall company. External newsletters are a friendly way of interacting with the public, making them feel involved in the company and yet at the same time delivering a sales message.

Internal newsletters are designed only for the staff. They can be lighter in tone and will feature individual and team successes. If they mention new products, it is only to inform everyone in the company; these newsletters are not sales documents. They may even contain some new policy or health and safety advice that is aimed squarely at employees, or perhaps feature some friendly 'who are you' features that help staff get to know each other.

The fact is that you can write persuasively for both of these media – but in different ways. You just need to be sure of your audience and focus.

When the audience is outside the organization you will need to stay clear of in-jokes, jargon, staff profiles (unless you are highlighting someone specifically for the public, such as a new customer care manager), internal awards (employee of the month) and any processes, procedures or codes of practice. Instead you will highlight any new products or services, any (feel-good) charity work, major business contracts won or awarded, complimentary letters and possibly a light feature such as a question and answer section or problem-solving slot. There is plenty of scope to use persuasive sales techniques to outline the benefits when describing your new products and services; the overall intention is to create interesting and informative reading for the customer that also feeds them ideas and further ways to continue to use your business. If you are producing this type of copy, make sure you keep a tight focus on what you want the endgame to be and then you can target your persuasion techniques towards this outcome.

For example, an external newsletter for a solicitor may include:

▶ welcome from the directors (to set the scene and say how busy the business has been. Notice there is a feel-good factor here: the message that you are in an exclusive 'club' of people who use this solicitor)

- introduction to any new solicitor or key member of staff (including photo to appear approachable – give contact details and positively invite your readers to contact them)

- successes (to demonstrate to the reader how successful the company is; this will also set up ideas in your reader's mind of what they might need)

- new legislation (to explain to the customer why they need you to feel safe)

- charity work (to show the customer that you are helping others and also the message that, if they use you, they are also indirectly helping others)

- highlighting a service (perhaps a feature on will writing or something 'useful' that will persuade the reader that they need you)

- ways to make contact (phone, email, address, with a warm invitation to do just that).

By contrast, the same solicitor may provide an internal newsletter for staff that could include:

- message from the director (motivating and encouraging, perhaps persuading certain desirable outcomes)

- which solicitors met their targets (performance targets)

- employee of the month (morale booster for staff)

- new Health and Safety legislation that comes in (information for staff to read)

- budget changes and VAT legislation and how they affect your business (company-specific information)

- new contracts won (and any that come to an end – an overview of the business)

- social club outings or company social meetings (spelling out the benefits of working there).

Both of these newsletters should be upbeat and encouraging but, whereas the external newsletter may have a fairly strong focus on sales (targeting will writing in the example above) and therefore be full of opportunities for persuasive writing techniques, the internal newsletter may still use these techniques but, to encourage staff to engage in the items, some items may be written by different members of staff and therefore the styles used throughout may vary.

Focus points

Persuasive writing can be incorporated into all aspects of business writing.

Provide your reader with motivation so that they undertake the action you want them to do.

Presentations offer a great opportunity for you to try out your persuasive techniques in a verbal and visual way.

There is more than one way to present a report, and persuasive techniques can be used to reassure customers and stakeholders that any issues are being dealt with appropriately.

Newsletters give the persuasive writer a great opportunity to practise their craft. The import issue is to identify the reader and the focus of the newsletter.

Case studies

Let's see how Leonie and Paul are faring.

Although Leonie has not undertaken any formal training yet, she is developing her skills by the day. She is not afraid to try new things and, although she knows that she is no expert, even she has to admit that she seems to have a flair for analysing text and playing around with words to create different reactions in others. She realizes that this could be a future career for her and she finds this thought exciting. She not only throws herself into writing the blog for the shoes but also starts to feel more like a member of staff, contributing towards other ideas. Only yesterday she sent a persuasive email to a work colleague to ask her if she would cover for her once a week because she is enrolling on a professional marketing course – and it worked! She is starting to realize that her writing skills can be used in many parts of the business, and, when she thinks back to that first CV, she cannot believe that she once thought that words and presentation were not that important. At the end of the second month Leonie's manager calls her into her office. She has some important news for Leonie. Not only has she decided to offer Leonie a permanent job in the department, but her blog is being followed by over 1,000 people and the figure is rising daily. Leonie is delighted and accepts. Now she can buy herself a smart briefcase and stride into the office, thinking 'I work here!'

Mr Pan's change of vision, to see how his company can grow but still stay true to its roots, is exactly what Paul had been working towards and it is a seminal moment for Pan's Haulage. Mr Pan had always thought that expansion meant moving away from his principles and selling out for more money, but Paul has persuaded him that there is a way that he can grow the business, create a secure future for his children and still have it remain very much the family firm. Paul has had to take a very slow persuasive style with Mr Pan as some of his ideas, although not unusual for most businesses, are somewhat radical for Mr Pan's family. It was important to gain Mr Pan's trust before he could even begin to make suggestions and now it seems that Mr Pan has come around to Paul's ideas in his own time – that is true persuasive skills at work. Mr Pan has told Paul that, if the business increases its profit (as it appears it might do soon), then Pan's Haulage will certainly be paying Paul a bonus to reward him for his efforts. Paul believes that so much is happening now that he is ready to start creating a new business plan for Mr Pan (the one they had been using was just a spreadsheet). Paul will also use the business plan to feed Mr Pan with further ideas. Paul, while keeping the website up and running, is now also starting to formulate ideas about a newsletter, which will be sent out to customers quarterly to tell them about what is happening at Pan's Haulage. He hopes that it will generate yet more interest and increase their profile, even if they offer it only to local businesses first. New software and printing technology means that Paul can create it very simply and cheaply. He knows that, yet again, he will have to persuade Mr Pan and his family, but he has more knowledge about that now and so begins to plan the newsletter and he has put Lizzie's picture on the front page. He can really see a future now for him in Pan's Haulage and he is excited by all the opportunities.

Next step

In this chapter we have looked at how persuasive writing can be integrated into almost any aspect of business. Yes, it is great for sales and advertising literature, but it is also effective in everyday writing such as letters and reports.

Learning to write persuasively is a journey rather than a destination and therefore we are all constantly learning. If you would like to research this exciting area further, there is a 'Further reading' section at the back of this book. Good luck and remember to keep writing!

Further Reading

Books and eBooks

Ashton, Robert, *Teach Yourself Successful Copywriting* (London: Hodder, 2012).

Bayan, Richard, *Words that Sell* (New York: McGraw-Hill, 2006).

Borg, James, *Persuasion: The Art of Influencing People* (Harlow: Prentice Hall, 2010).

Camp, Lindsay, *Can I Change Your Mind* (London: A & C Black, 2007).

Canavor, Natalie and Meirowitz, Claire, *Some Essential Grammar Tips for More Effective Business Writing* (eBook: Financial Times Press, 2010).

Frederick, Peter, *Persuasive Writing* (London: Pearson Business, 2011).

Graham, Daniel and Graham, Judith, *Can Do Writing: Proven Ten-Step System for Fast and Effective Business Writing* (eBook: Wiley, 2009).

Levine, Robert, *The Power of Persuasion: How We Are Bought and Sold* (Hoboken, NJ: John Wiley & Sons, 2006).

Maslen, Andy, *The Copywriting Sourcebook: How to Write Better Copy Faster – for Everything from Ads to Websites* (London: Marshall Cavendish, 2010).

Redish, Janice, *Letting Go of the Words* (Waltham, MA: Morgan Kaufmann, 2007).

Sant, Tom, *Persuasive Business Proposals* (Kindle edition: AMACOM Media EU, 2009).

Vickers, Amanda and Bavister, Steve, *Teach Yourself: Present with Impact and Confidence* (London: Hodder, 2010).

Helpful contacts

Chartered Institute of Marketing – www.cim.co.uk

Copywriting Institute – www.thecopywritinginstitute.com

Institute of Copywriting – www.inst.org/copy/

Institute of Sales and Marketing Management – www.ismm.co.uk

Index

actions to try
  argumentation, cohesiveness
    in 109
  focus, endgame and 34
  misconceptions about persuasive
    writing 3, 4, 5, 6
  new truths 17, 19, 22
  techniques that work 51, 56
adopters as target group 72, 75
advertorials 105–7
AIDA (attention, interest, desire,
  action) formula 116–17
apologies 22–3
appearance, importance of
  92–5
appraisal paperwork 150–2
argumentation, cohesiveness in
  99–112
  action to try 109
  case studies 111–12
  diagnostic test 100–1
  focus points 110
  key ideas 103, 106, 108
  next step 112
  points to remember 101, 103,
    105, 107, 110
assumptions 73–4
attention-catching 6–7, 116

benefits, sales copy and setting
  out of 124–5
blogs 140–1
business
  business planning 148–50
  motivational techniques
    in 95–6
  see also work situations, persuasive
    techniques for

case studies
  argumentation, cohesiveness in
    111–12
  focus, endgame and 45–6
  misconceptions about persuasive
    writing 12–13
  motivational writing 97–8
  new truths 28–9
  persuasive language 81
  sales copy, production of 127–8
  techniques that work 64–5
  web copy, persuasive techniques
    for 143–4
  work situations, persuasive
    techniques for 160–1
celebrity endorsements 23–4
chunking web copy 132–4
cohesive argumentation 102–5
  example of 104–5
  reasons for use of 103
collaboration with readers 56
confident decision-making 4–5
connections, searching out 18–19
consistency 60–1, 79
contacts 164
customers, truths about 119–22
cutting and rethinking web pages
  138–40

deadlines 39–41
desire 117
diagnostic tests
  argumentation, cohesiveness
    in 100–1
  focus, endgame and 32–3
  misconceptions about persuasive
    writing 2–3
  motivational writing 84–5

new truths 16–17
persuasive language 68–9
sales copy, production of 114–15
techniques that work 48–9
web copy, persuasive techniques for 130–1
work situations, persuasive techniques for 146–7

early majority as target group 72, 75
emotions, tapping into 51–3
energetic words 89
engagement with readers 35–7
envy 53

flattery 20–2
focus, endgame and 31–46
    action to try 34
    case studies 45–6
    diagnostic test 32–3
    focus points 44
    key ideas 37, 38, 41
    next step 46
    points to remember 33, 34, 36, 41, 43, 44
focus points
    argumentation, cohesiveness in 110
    focus, endgame and 44
    misconceptions about persuasive writing 12
    motivational writing 96–7
    new truths 28
    persuasive language 80
    sales copy, production of 126–7
    techniques that work 64
    web copy, persuasive techniques for 142–3
    work situations, persuasive techniques for 160
forgiveness seeking 22–3
free offers, customers' liking for 120–1
further reading 163

goal setting 39–41
greed 52
grouping of words and phrases 79–80
guilt 53

headlines 125–6
helpfulness 7–8
herd instincts 61–2
highlighting important words 126
'hook'
    on web pages 135–7
    in writing 77

impact, starting with 77–8
importance, levels of 34
informativeness, trust and 11
innovators as target group 72, 75
interest 117
Internet use 132

key ideas
    argumentation, cohesiveness in 103, 106, 108
    focus, endgame and 37, 38, 41
    misconceptions about persuasive writing 8, 9, 11
    motivational writing 87, 91, 96
    new truths 20, 21, 23, 24
    persuasive language 71, 73, 75
    sales copy, production of 119, 122, 125
    techniques that work 52, 53, 55
    web copy, persuasive techniques for 134, 136, 140, 142
    work situations, persuasive techniques for 150, 153, 155
killer headlines 125–6
knowledgability, choice and 10–11

late majority as target group 72, 75
likeableness 5–6
links on web pages 135–7

magnetism 23–4
metaphors, use of 59–60
misconceptions about persuasive
        writing 1–13
    actions to try 3, 4, 5, 6
    case studies 12–13
    diagnostic test 2–3
    focus points 12
    key ideas 8, 9, 11
    next step 13
    points to remember 5, 7, 12
mistakes, dealing with 22–3
motivation 34, 86–7
    creation of, importance of 87–8
motivational phrases 90–1
motivational words 89–90
motivational writing 83–98
    case studies 97–8
    diagnostic test 84–5
    focus points 96–7
    introduction of 95–6
    key ideas 87, 91, 96
    next step 98
    points to remember 85, 87, 88,
        90, 95
    at work 95–6
multiple sales strategy, creation of
        118–19

negativity 6–7
new truths 15–29
    actions to try 17, 19, 22
    case studies 28–9
    diagnostic test 16–17
    focus points 28
    key ideas 20, 21, 23, 24
    next step 29
    points to remember 18, 26, 27
newsletters 157–60
numbers, sales copy and use
        of 126

overconfidence 7–8

perceptions, values and 60
personal endorsements 122
persuasive language 67–82
    case studies 81
    diagnostic test 68–9
    focus points 80
    key ideas 71, 73, 75
    next step 82
    points to remember 69, 70, 71, 74,
        76, 78, 79
persuasiveness
    connections and 19–20
    crafting endgame arguments 42–3
    idea of 3–4
    language use and 74–5
    motivational writing and 95–6
    power of 17–18
    realism about limits of 49
points to remember
    argumentation, cohesiveness in 101,
        103, 105, 107, 110
    focus, endgame and 33, 34, 36, 41,
        43, 44
    misconceptions about persuasive
        writing 5, 7, 12
    motivational writing 85, 87, 88,
        90, 95
    new truths 18, 26, 27
    persuasive language 69, 70, 71, 74,
        76, 78, 79
    sales copy, production of 115, 116,
        118, 119, 123, 124, 126
    techniques that work 49, 51, 55,
        56, 57
    web copy, persuasive techniques for
        131, 132, 135, 137, 141
    work situations, persuasive
        techniques for 148, 149, 152,
        154, 157
positivity 57
presentations 153–5
pricing, customers' liking for
        reasonableness in 121

'problem', sales copy and relating to 123–4
problem-solving 55
pushiness 7–8

readers
  collaboration with 56
  leading (not misleading) 109–10
  risk minimization for 62–3
  truths about 119–22
  understanding about and engagement with 35–7
reading, writing and 71–3
reassuring words 89
reciprocity 24–6
recommendations 19–20, 53
reflective light 23–4
repetition 54–5
reports 155–7
research, importance of 37–8
responsibility in writing 109–10
rewrites, avoidance of 41–2
risk minimization for customers 62–3

safety, customers' liking for 121
sales copy, production of 113–28
  case studies 127–8
  diagnostic test 114–15
  focus points 126–7
  key ideas 119, 122, 125
  next step 128
  points to remember 115, 116, 118, 119, 123, 124, 126
sales data 115–16
sales strategy 118–19
scanning web pages 134–5
selling benefits 50–1
selling yourself 122–3
similes, use of 59–60
simplicity 62, 78–9
  customers' liking for 120

SMART (specific, measurable, agreed, realistic, timed) goals 40–1, 151–2
sociability 18–19
speed of gratification, customers' liking for 120
split testing 73
Steps to Success programme 63
stories, use of 59–60
structured argumentation 107–8
structured web copy 132–4
success, celebration of 43–4
sweeteners, offers of 63–4

target groups 72–3
techniques that work 47–66
  actions to try 51, 56
  case studies 64–5
  diagnostic test 48–9
  focus points 64
  key ideas 52, 53, 55
  next step 66
  points to remember 49, 51, 55, 56, 57
temptation, gratification and 61
testimonials 121–2
thinking, renewed ways of 17–18
time management 33–4
traditionalists as target group 73, 75
trust 11, 53, 56, 122, 123

value, customers' liking for knowledge of 121
values, perceptions and 60

wants and needs 8–9
web copy, persuasive techniques for 129–44
  case studies 143–4
  diagnostic test 130–1
  focus points 142–3
  key ideas 134, 136, 140, 142
  next step 144

points to remember 131, 132, 135,
    137, 141
websites and books, comparisons of
    132–3
wordplay 109
work situations, persuasive techniques
    for 145–62
  case studies 160–1
  diagnostic test 146–7
  focus points 160
  key ideas 150, 153, 155
  next step 162
  points to remember 148, 149, 152,
    154, 157

working, renewed ways of
    17–18
writing
  analysis of 76
  business letters 152–3
  communication tool 70–1
  tightness and focus in
    41–2
  wonder of 69–70

yes responses, encouragement
    of 58–9
'you', sales copy and use
    of 126

Notes